Goa Travel Gu

Insider Insights, Beach Escapes, and
Must-See Attractions for a Memorable
Goa Adventure- Includes a 7-Day
Itinerary

By Larry E. Miller

1

Copyright

Introduction: My Visit to Goa

A place that seamlessly blends the fabric of history, culture, and natural beauty is nestled along the sun-kissed shores of the Arabian Sea. My adventure starts here, in the alluring embrace of Goa.

A pleasant wind laced with the aroma of the ocean greeted me as I walked onto the tarmac at Goa's Dabolim Airport. My senses were tingling with excitement as I anticipated finding this coastal paradise. With swaying palms and turquoise waves softly lapping at the shoreline, the landscape that appeared in front of me was nothing short of a tropical utopia. This first glance at Goa set the stage for an incredible journey.

While navigating the quaint streets of Goa, I found myself in a setting where Indian traditions and Portuguese heritage coexist together. The buildings' architecture told tales of a bygone age, with colonial influences seen in the exteriors of churches, forts, and meandering lanes. I was struck by the Baroque splendor of the Basilica of Bom Jesus as I stood in front of it; it is a symbol of the cultural mix that characterizes Goa.

I followed the coastline as my adventure progressed, learning about the riches of each beach, from Baga's exuberant energy to Palolem's crescent bay's serenity. While the gorgeous sands of Morjim appeared like a tranquil haven surrounded by nature, Anjuna's bohemian spirit pulled me in.

Goa's charm extends beyond its beaches. Old cathedrals and temples revealed tales of devotion and heritage, while crowded local markets provided a window into the Goans' daily life. Each vendor appeared to tell secrets of a region steeped in tradition, from the aromatic spices of the Mapusa Market to the colorful textiles of the Anjuna Flea Market.

And then there was the evening, which was an eclectic mix of beachside fun and reverberating music. Goa's nights are as colorful as its sunny days, from the beats of local musicians at small clubs to the famous electronic music scene.

But maybe the most fascinating part of my trip was the chance meetings I had with locals. The conversation flowed as easily as the ocean's waters. These conversations improved my comprehension of the soul of Goa, from fishermen telling stories of the day's catch to artists revealing the techniques behind their trades.

In this guide, I invite you to step into my footsteps as I traverse through Goa's diverse landscapes, savor its flavors, and immerse myself in its cultural tapestry. Goa's many attractions guarantee an amazing journey, whether you're looking for the ideal beach, the heart of a busy market, or the peace of a peaceful hideaway.

So gather your curiosity and go on this exploration as we explore Goa's soul together. Goa is a wonderful fusion of history, nature, and the welcoming embrace of its people. Goa is prepared to capture your heart and soul as you embark on your adventure.

Table of Contents

Chapter 1: Introduction to Goa

Welcome to India's Tropical Paradise

A symphony of sensations that characterize this coastal sanctuary greets you as soon as you set foot on Goa's sun-kissed shores. Travelers from all over the globe are drawn to India's tropical paradise, which is known for its golden beaches, verdant landscapes, and colorful culture. Goa serves as a shining example of the fascinating variety that India has to offer with its combination of history, leisure, and festivities.

A Coastal Canvas

Goa, which is located on India's west coast, has a coastline that spans more than 100 kilometers. The tides' ebb and flow determine the rhythm of life here. Goa's shores can accommodate every mood, whether you're looking for the frantic adrenaline of crowded beaches or the serene beauty of secluded coves.

A Fusion of Culture

Goa's history as a Portuguese colony, a heritage that has left an unmistakable stamp on the state's architecture, food, and way of life, is a key part of the state's identity. The colonial-era churches in the state, where elaborate designs and historical importance merge, serve as living memorials to the state's colorful history.

Beaches that Stand Out

Every beach in Goa has its identity. These beaches provide more than simply gorgeous landscapes, with Anjuna's lively markets and nightlife, Palolem's peaceful stretches, and Baga's electrifying vitality. They are gateways into the heart of Goa's unique spirit, greeting visitors with open arms and providing experiences ranging from peaceful sunbathing to daring water sports.

Gastronomic Delights

Goa's cuisine is a tapestry made of influences that are as diverse as its history. As local markets provide insight into the components that form Goan tastes, the air is filled with the enticing perfume of spices. Every dish, whether it be spicy curries or delicate seafood, celebrates the region's abundant resources and rich culinary heritage.

Celebrations and Festivals

Festivals that combine Indian traditions with local customs may be seen throughout Goa's diverse cultural calendar. Holi's vivid hues, Carnival's colorful parades, and Diwali's spiritual fervor all find their manifestations against Goa's varied landscape.

Local Hospitality

People are perhaps Goa's most alluring feature. The laid-back character of the region is reflected in the friendly hospitality of the inhabitants in Goa. Every tourist is welcomed like an old friend, and conversations flow as easily as the waves.

I cordially encourage you to immerse yourself in the heart of Goa via the pages of this guide. Goa is a place that seduces with its beautiful beaches, enriches with its rich cultural heritage, and charms with the friendliness of its inhabitants. Prepare to be mesmerized by the beauty

13

that emerges at every turn as you travel through this tropical paradise.

Why Goa is a Great Travel Destination

Goa, which is tucked away on India's southwest coast, is proof positive of the pull of the unexpected. This little coastal state is more than just a blip on the map; it's a universe unto itself, bursting with a vivid tapestry of experiences that entice tourists from all over the world. Goa's distinctive fusion of history, leisure, and celebration makes it a great destination for all types of travelers, from its sun-drenched beaches to its rich cultural heritage.

A Paradise For Beach Lovers
Goa's beaches, which span more than 100 kilometers of coastline, are fantasies come true. You'll find your sanctuary here whether you're looking for the hum of bustle or the calm of seclusion. In addition to serving as a background, the unending expanse of sand serves as a

venue for a variety of activities, from the thrills of water sports to the serenity of beachside yoga sessions.

Cultural Kaleidoscope

Goa's rich history has shaped who it is now. For more than 400 years, the state was a Portuguese colony, and its architecture, food, and way of life all brilliantly reflect this past. Every nook and cranny of Goa tells a tale of its history, from the imposing churches of Old Goa, a UNESCO World Heritage Site, to the colorful street markets that line the streets.

Festivals that Define Goa

Goa savors life rather than merely celebrating it. The state's calendar is packed with vivid festivities and colorful festivals that reflect its distinctive cultural blend. Goa's festivals highlight its rich traditions and friendly spirit, from the raucous pre-Lenten Carnival to the ornate Diwali festivities.

A Gastronomic Odyssey

Goa is a true heaven for the taste buds of food lovers. This coastal paradise's food pleasingly combines tastes, reflecting on its colonial heritage and the abundant local vegetables. Every meal in Goa is a study of its rich culinary heritage, from the smoky vindaloos to the delicate aromas of freshly caught seafood.

Beyond the Nightlife

Goa's nightlife comes to life as the sun sets in a magnificent display of lights, music, and excitement. A diversified and electrifying environment is created in the clubs and beach shacks by the music that fills them. The state's cultural performances, art galleries, and live events provide a look into its creative soul beyond the rhythms.

Hospitality Beyond Measure

The kindness of its people is what gives Goa its heart and soul. The hospitality and laid-back nature of Goans are well-known. You'll be greeted with open arms and friendly smiles whether you're engaging in discussion with locals at a beachside hut or taking part in cultural festivities.

I welcome you to learn more about Goa's many aspects that make it a great travel destination in this guide. Goa delivers an experience that remains long after you leave its shores, whether you're looking for sun-drenched excursions, cultural exploration, or vivacious festivals. So, go off on this adventure with an open heart, prepared to soak in Goa's beauty.

Goa's Rich History

Goa's attractiveness is rooted in its enthralling history, a tale that unfolds over the ages and leaves an indelible stamp on its landscape and culture, beyond the glistening sands and vivid festivities. The echoes of the past can be heard in every nook of this coastal sanctuary, from ancient dynasties to colonial conquests, beckoning tourists to set out on a trip through time.

Origins and Dynasties of Antiquity

Goa saw the rise and collapse of empires long before European explorers set foot on its shores. Goa is mentioned in ancient Indian scriptures dating back to the Mauryan Empire, which is where the region's history began. This region was ruled by the Satavahanas, Chalukyas, and Kadambas in that order, and each left its mark on the architecture and cultural fabric.

Colonial Tapestry: Portuguese Legacy

The entrance of the Portuguese in the 16th century was a significant turning point in the history of Goa. The colonists had a lasting effect, ushering in a time that profoundly shaped Goa's identity. The grand churches and cathedrals of Old Goa are examples of colonial architecture, a combination of European and Indian traditions. One of them is the Basilica of Bom Jesus, a UNESCO World Heritage Site that contains St. Francis Xavier's mortal remains.

Cultural Crossroads and Religious Heritage

Additionally, the colonial era cleared the stage for the blending of cultures and the spread of Christianity in

Goa. Goa had a turbulent period as the Eastern Inquisition's headquarters, but it eventually emerged as a furnace of devotion and faith. With its stunning architecture and deep symbolism, the Se Cathedral, which is dedicated to St. Catherine, serves as an inspirational testament to this heritage.

Contemporary Advances and Liberation

With its independence from colonial domination in the 20th century, Goa's history saw yet another crucial turning point. Goa's freedom in 1961 opened a pivotal chapter in its history, regaining its independence and defining its contemporary character.

A Living Heritage

You'll discover as you delve into Goa's historical riches that the state's everyday life is infused with history, making it clear that it isn't relegated to textbooks and museums. Goa's rich history is woven into its present, producing a pleasing tapestry of past and present, from the vibrant festivals that celebrate its traditions to the way its architecture recounts stories of a bygone age.

I cordially welcome you to go back in time with me as you peruse the pages of Goa's history with this guide. You'll learn about the layers that contribute to Goa's current allure via its compelling tales and architectural wonders. You'll discover that Goa's history is not simply a narrative of the past, but an essential element of the vivid present that you're about to experience, whether you're roaming through the hallways of old churches or strolling through the cobbled streets of historic towns.

Chapter 2: Essential Travel Planning

Best Time to Experience Goa's Charms

Goa is an Indian state on the Arabian Sea's western coast. It is well-known for its stunning beaches, relaxed way of life, and colorful culture. Your interests and preferences will determine the perfect time to visit Goa.

Winter (February to November)
The most popular time to visit Goa is during the winter months. The weather is good, with temperatures ranging from 20 to 30 degrees Celsius on average. This is the best time to visit the beach since the beaches are less crowded and the water is warm and clear. During the winter, Goa hosts several festivals and events, including Christmas and New Year's Eve festivities, the Sunburn Festival, and the Goa Carnival.

Here are some of the benefits and drawbacks of visiting Goa in the winter:

Pros
The weather is pleasant.
Beaches with fewer people
There are several festivals and events.

Cons
Peak season means greater pricing.
More people in general
It may become humid at times.

Monsoon Season (June to September)
If you don't mind a little rain, the monsoon season is another great time to visit Goa. The monsoon rains transform the landscape into lush greenery, and the beaches become less busy. There are also some excellent options for water sports like surfing and kayaking.

Here are some of the benefits and drawbacks of visiting Goa during the monsoon season:

Pros

Beaches with fewer people

Excellent water sports opportunities

luscious greenery

Cons

Wet weather

Can be humid

Some roads may be closed

Summer Months (March to May)

The summer months in Goa are hot and humid, with temperatures averaging 30 to 35 degrees Celsius. This is not the best time to visit if you want to go on a beach vacation, but it might be a nice time to visit if you want to learn about the state's culture and history.

Here are some of the benefits and drawbacks of visiting Goa in the summer:

Pros

Fewer people

Lower prices

It's a good time to learn about culture and history.

Cons

Hot and humid weather

Not suitable for beach trips.

Off-season (October)

If you are searching for a shoulder season vacation, October is a terrific time to visit Goa. With typical temperatures ranging from 25 to 30 degrees Celsius, the weather remains nice. In addition, there are fewer visitors in Goa around October, so you can enjoy the beaches and other attractions without having to contend with crowds.

Here are some of the benefits and drawbacks of visiting Goa in October:

Pros

The weather is pleasant.

Fewer people

It's a great time to visit the beaches.

Cons

There aren't as many festivals or events.

Some establishments may be closed.

Your interests and preferences will determine the perfect time to visit Goa. If you want to go on a beach vacation, the winter months are the greatest time to visit. Monsoon season might also be a nice time to visit if you don't mind a little rain. If you want to learn more about Goa's culture and history, the summer months are a fantastic time to visit.

Packing Essentials for Your Goa Adventure

In addition to anticipation, planning your trip to Goa entails meticulous packing to make sure you have everything you need for a comfortable and fun excursion. This comprehensive packing guide for your

Goa vacation covers everything from beach basics to cultural excursions.

Beach Gear and Sun Protection
Swimwear: Bring a range of swimwear to accommodate various beach activities, from relaxing to participating in water sports.

Sunscreen: The sun in Goa may be quite harsh. Choose a sunscreen with a high SPF to protect your skin from UV radiation.

Hat and Sunglasses: Protecting your face and eyes from the sun requires wearing a wide-brimmed hat and UV-protective sunglasses.

Beach mat or cover-up: A thin towel or sarong may be used as a beach mat.

Sandals or Flip-Flops: Comfortable and water-friendly footwear is ideal for navigating the sandy shores.

Footwear and Clothing

Light, Breathable Clothing: Goa's climate calls for light and breathable clothing. Pack t-shirts, skirts, and shorts made of comfy cotton.

Cover-Ups: When visiting temples and churches, take into account wearing cover-ups or long scarves to observe local customs.

Walking Shoes: For touring marketplaces, historical sites, and nature trails, you must have a pair of suitable walking shoes.

Evening Attire: If you plan on experiencing Goa's vibrant nightlife, pack a few smart-casual outfits for evening activities.

Rain Gear (Monsoon Season): If visiting during the monsoon, a compact raincoat or umbrella will come in handy.

Essentials and Electronics

Travel adapters: Goa makes use of Type D power outlets, so make sure you pack the right one for recharging your electronics.

Camera: Use a camera or smartphone to capture beautiful landscapes and thriving culture.

Portable Charger: Stay powered up, especially when exploring away from accommodations.

Travel Documents: Be sure to include your passport, visa, and any necessary proof of travel insurance.

First Aid and Health
Medication: Bring a basic first aid kit for minor injuries, as well as any prescription drugs you need.

Insect Repellent: Protect yourself from mosquitoes, especially during the evenings.

Hydration: In the tropical environment, having a refillable water bottle will be very helpful.

Miscellaneous Essentials

Cash: Even though many locations accept credit cards, having some local money might be useful, particularly in rural locations.

Reusable Bag: A compact, foldable bag is ideal for storing everyday necessities and mementos.

Guidebook or Maps: Despite digital navigation, having a physical map or guidebook can be beneficial for exploring.

Keep in mind that practicality and comfort are essential for enabling you to completely immerse yourself in the beauty and experiences that are in store for you. Your well-packed bag will be your dependable travel companion whether you're seeing historic places, relaxing on the beach, or indulging in local delicacies.

Visas and Entry Requirements

Foreign nationals visiting Goa, India, must have a valid passport as well as a valid visa unless they are citizens of visa-exempt countries or nations who may receive a visa on arrival or an e-visa online.

Visa-free Travel

Nepalese and Bhutanese citizens do not need a visa or passport to enter India (unless they are traveling from China, Hong Kong, Pakistan, or Macau). These nationalities have no restrictions on their stay in India and may even work there.

Maldives nationals do not need a visa to stay for up to 90 days.

Overseas Indian Citizens/People of Indian Origin

Nationals possessing an Overseas Citizen of India registration certificate or a Person having an Indian Origin Card are exempt from visa requirements. Please keep in mind that citizens of Afghanistan, Bangladesh, Bhutan, China, Nepal, or Pakistan do not have Overseas Citizenship.

Visa on Arrival

Japanese, South Korean, and UAE nationals may apply for a visa on arrival (VOA) at the airports of Bengaluru, Chennai, Delhi, Hyderabad, Kolkata, and Mumbai. The visa is valid for up to 60 days and is issued for certain purposes such as business, tourism, medical treatment, and conferences.

Please keep in mind that a national cannot apply for a visa on arrival if he or she, or any of his or her parents or grandparents, was born in or are permanent residents of Pakistan.

E-visa

Nationals of certain countries, including those entitled to visas on arrival, may apply for an e-visa. There are three sorts of e-visas: e-tourist visas, e-business visas, and

31

e-medical visas. An e-visa application must be submitted four calendar days before the date of arrival.

Tourism Entry Requirements

In addition to being a citizen of a visa-exempt nation, you must also fulfill specific entry conditions to visit Goa for tourist purposes. These prerequisites are as follows:

A valid passport with at least six months remaining validity.

A return or onward ticket.

Evidence of enough cash to sustain your stay in India.

Other papers, such as a letter of invitation from a friend or family in India, may also be required.

Customs

When you arrive in Goa, you will have to clear customs. Any things you bring into the nation must be declared, and you may be required to pay duty on some items.

Prohibited Items

Certain things, such as alcohol, cigarettes, and narcotics, are prohibited from being carried into India. Before traveling to Goa, you should thoroughly review the customs requirements.

For the latest information, please visit India's Bureau of Immigration website at https://boi.gov.in/ or the Indian visa online site at https://indianvisaonline.gov.in/

Currency, Banking, and Payment Tips

Understanding the local currency, banking options, and payment customs is crucial as you get ready for your trip to Goa if you want to travel smoothly and without anxiety. Making the most of your stay in this vivacious seaside paradise will be made possible by navigating the financial terrain.

Currency in Goa

The Indian Rupee, abbreviated as INR, serves as both Goa and India's official currency. It comes in a range of denominations, including coins and bills. You can manage transactions more comfortably if you are familiar with the money and its denominations.

Using ATMs and Banking

ATMs: Throughout Goa, ATMs are easily accessible in both urban and tourist regions. Major international credit and debit cards are accepted there. To prevent any problems using your card, don't forget to let your bank know about your vacation intentions.

Currency Exchange: You can exchange foreign currency at authorized currency exchange counters, banks, and certain hotels. To guarantee you obtain the greatest value, it's advised to check prices on a visa.

Banks: Goa is home to a network of financial institutions that provide a variety of services. Although banks are typically open during business hours on weekdays, it is best to call ahead to confirm.

Tips for Payment

Cash & Cards: Although cards are often accepted, particularly at hotels, fine dining places, and shops, it is still essential to have some cash on hand for smaller businesses, local markets, and transportation. To prevent any problems using your card while traveling, let your bank know.

Tipping: In Goa, tipping is customary. Although not required, it is welcomed. If service costs are not already included, it is typical to tip 10% to 15% in restaurants.

Negotiating: Smaller shops and local marketplaces have a culture of haggling. Be courteous while haggling and bear in mind that the purpose of the process is to make friends and have fun.

Small Denominations: Having small denominations of cash can be helpful for local transportation, street food, and small purchases.

Local Markets: When visiting local markets or street stalls, it is important to have cash on hand since card payment options may not always be available.

Beach Shacks: Especially for minor purchases, many beach shacks and other tiny businesses may only accept cash.

Security and Safety
Wallet Safety: Exercise caution when handling cash and cards. To keep your possessions safe, use a money belt or a travel wallet with a lock.

Backup Options: It's a good idea to have backup cards or travelers' checks in case of any unexpected issues.

Online Transactions: Be cautious to use a secure network and reputable websites when doing any kind of online business.

In this section, you've gained insights into managing your finances while exploring Goa. Being well-prepared, from currency exchange to payment procedures, guarantees that you can concentrate on taking in Goa's lively culture, breathtaking landscapes, and kind hospitality. Strike a balance between using cash and credit cards, keep up with available banking options, and adopt local customs for tipping and bartering. Now that your financial concerns are taken care of, you may completely enjoy Goa's beauty and allure.

Getting to Goa

Starting your trip to Goa is an exciting step toward seeing this coastal paradise's attractions. Understanding the numerous transportation options and making wise judgments can set the stage for an unforgettable experience, whether you're traveling by plane, train, or road.

Arriving by Air

The primary entry point to Goa is Dabolim Airport, which is situated in Vasco da Gama. An international airport that serves both domestic and international flights is this one. Upon arrival, you'll discover several amenities, such as baggage claim, currency exchange kiosks, and transportation options to get you where you're going. Visit the official Dabolim Airport website at https://www.aai.aero/en/airports/goa for additional details.

Domestic Flights: There are several direct flights from important Indian cities to Goa. Airlines regularly provide services linking well-known locations including Mumbai, Delhi, Bangalore, Kolkata, and Chennai. Because flight times might vary, choose the one that best fits your itinerary.

International Flights: The Dabolim AirPort also acts as a point of entry for visitors from other countries. Travelers from around the globe may reach Goa with ease because of the availability of direct flights from a few international locations.

Arriving by Train

Railway Stations in Goa: Margao (Madgaon) and Vasco da Gama are the two main railway stations in Goa. Regular rail services connect both stations to important Indian cities and towns. Visit https://www.irctc.co.in/nget/train-search, the official Indian Railways website, for further information on train timetables, reservations, and tickets.

Konkan Railway: The Western Ghats and the seashore are both passed through on the route of the Konkan Railway. This picturesque road offers an amazing travel experience and is known for its spectacular vistas.

Arriving by Road
National Highways: A network of national highways connects Goa to nearby states and cities. Depending on your tastes and convenience, you may choose between self-driving, rental automobiles, and even bus services.

Bus Services: Several state-run and private bus services connect Goa with surrounding states. There are day and night buses that provide varied degrees of luxury and amenities. You may check websites like https://www.redbus.in/ or https://www.goabus.in/ for bus timetables and reservations.

Ferry Services

Waterways: Goa is accessible by water as a result of the abundance of its rivers and estuaries. A distinctive and picturesque arrival is made possible by ferry services, which link various regions of the state.

Arrangements for Arrival

Advance Bookings: Whether you're arriving by air, rail, or road, it's advisable to book your tickets in advance, especially during peak travel seasons.

Local Transportation: To get you to your accommodations after your arrival, there are taxis, auto-rickshaws, and app-based cab services available. To guarantee a fair price, haggle over fares or choose metered options.

Navigation Apps: Utilize navigation apps on your smartphone to help you find your way to your destination once you've arrived in Goa.

Airport Transfers: For the convenience of its visitors, several hotels provide airport transfer services. If you want to know whether this service is offered, ask about your accommodations.

Local Advice: Upon arrival, don't be afraid to seek advice from locals or tourist information offices. On the top routes, transportation options, and local advice, they may provide insightful information.

The means of transportation that best fits your interests and timetable should be taken into account when you arrange your arrival in Goa. Your trip to this coastal jewel will be the start of a memorable discovery of culture, beauty, and adventure, regardless of whether you decide to fly, ride the rails, take the road, or even set sail.

Moving Around Goa

The next thrilling part of your vacation starts when you reach Goa and start discovering the numerous wonders this place has to offer. Thanks to a wide range of transportation options in Goa that may accommodate all tastes and budgets, getting around the city is a snap. Here is a comprehensive guide to traveling around this coastal beauty, from hectic cities to peaceful beaches.

Options for Local Transport
Taxis and Auto-Rickshaws: Taxis and auto-rickshaws are readily available in urban areas and tourist hotspots. Although taxis often have fixed meters, it's a good idea to haggle over prices or get a quote before you leave.

Buses: Goa has a vast network of public and private buses that link the state's many regions. Although buses are a cheap choice, they may not always be the most convenient and time-efficient.

Motorbike and Scooter Rentals: Renting a motorbike or scooter is a popular choice among travelers who wish to explore Goa at their own pace. The state is filled with rental companies that provide a variety of options for those who like riding two-wheel.

Cycling: For those who care about the environment and are daring, cycling is an excellent way to discover the beautiful landscapes of Goa. You may hire bicycles from local shops, and many places have designated cycling trails.

App-Based Ride Services
Taxis: Since Goa has adopted app-based travel services, it's simple to reserve a cab on your smartphone. In well-known cities and towns, popular services like Uber and Ola are available.

Scooter Rentals: To make it easier for you to reserve a scooter, several scooter rental firms now provide app-based booking services.

Exploring Different Regions

North Goa: For enjoying the lively beaches and nightlife of North Goa, buses, taxis, and rental two-wheelers are all great options. Road signs are legible and well-maintained.

South Goa: Much like North Goa, South Goa has a variety of transportation options. Generally speaking, the pace is slower, which is perfect for unhurried exploring.

Navigating the Roads

Driving: If you plan to drive, keep in mind that Goans drive on the left side of the road. Drive carefully and be prepared for sporadic traffic since road conditions might change.

Parking facilities are available at the majority of accommodations. Make sure you are informed of the rules for parking and costs if you want to explore busier locations.

Ferry Crossings

River Crossings: Ferries are used to traverse the rivers in Goa, offering both a distinctive travel experience and a practical means to go from one side to the other.

Local Insights

Local Advice: Don't hesitate to ask locals for directions or recommendations. Goans are renowned for their gracious hospitality and openness to assistance.

Google Maps: Utilize navigation apps on your smartphone to find your way around. Using Google Maps to find locations and calculate journey times is quite helpful.

Safety Considerations

Helmets: Always wear a helmet while operating a motorcycle or scooter. Not only is it necessary by law, but it's also very important for your protection.

Keep Documents Handy: Keep photocopies of your passport, visa, and other important documents handy when you're on the road.

Local Experiences

Beach Shacks: Many beaches feature little shacks that provide food, drinks, and even rental gear, enhancing your beach adventures.

Scenic Routes: Whenever possible, choose scenic routes. Going off the beaten path might result in surprising discoveries since Goa's landscapes are so varied.

Keep in mind that the travel itself is a crucial component of the experience as you explore Goa's captivating places. The ease and flexibility of transportation options guarantee that your tour of Goa is as compelling as its cultural and natural attractions, whether you're traveling through palm-fringed roads, admiring spectacular ocean vistas, or visiting charming towns.

Chapter 3: Accommodation

Budget-friendly Accommodations

As you embark on your journey to Goa, a diverse realm of accommodation options unveils itself, tailored to suit a spectrum of budgets and preferences. For those seeking a blend of comfort and budget-consciousness, Goa offers a myriad of budget-friendly choices. These options not only ensure convenience but also provide an opportunity to fully experience the coastal charm without straining your finances. Whether you're a solo explorer, a couple on a romantic getaway, or a group of friends in pursuit of adventure, Goa's budget-friendly accommodations lay the foundation for an enriching journey.

Guesthouses and Hostels

Guesthouses: Scattered across Goa, guesthouses offer simplicity and comfort at reasonable rates. These cozy establishments range from unassuming to charming, often equipped with essential amenities. Whether nestled within urban hubs or nestled near renowned beaches, guesthouses provide a comfortable and budget-friendly abode.

Recommendations

"Casa de Goa" in Calangute Beach: Known for its affordable rates and warm hospitality. Website: www.casadegoa.com, Phone: +91-832-2276081.

"Sai Residency" in Anjuna: Offers a tranquil escape with easy access to the beach. Phone: +91-992-359-0924.

Hostels

A favorite among solo travelers and backpackers, hostels foster camaraderie and cost-effectiveness. In Goa, well-maintained hostels offer dormitory-style accommodations, shared lounges, and communal kitchens, creating a vibrant atmosphere.

Recommendations:

"The Hostel Crowd" in Anjuna: Known for its social events and cozy environment. Website: www.thehostelcrowd.com, Phone: +91-976-555-3445.

"Jungle by thehostelcrowd" in Vagator: Offers a rustic jungle setting and vibrant community. Website: www.junglehostel.in, Phone: +91-976-555-3445.

Beach Huts and Shacks

Beach Huts

For a closer connection to nature, opt for rustic beach huts along Goa's coastlines. Constructed with bamboo and thatch, these huts offer basic amenities and an immersive coastal experience.

Recommendations

"Palm Grove Beach Huts" in Palolem Beach: Known for its tranquil ambiance and direct beach access. Phone: +91-982-212-2447.

"Sundown Beach Huts" in Agonda Beach: Offers a serene beachfront setting. Phone: +91-954-500-0042.

Beach Shacks

Embrace the beach lifestyle with budget-friendly beach shacks that offer comfortable lodging right on the sands.

Recommendations
"Britto's Beach Shack" in Baga Beach: Renowned for its laid-back vibe and beachfront location. Phone: +91-982-214-5042.

"Fisherman's Wharf" in Majorda Beach: Offers a delightful beachside dining experience. Phone: +91-960-441-7544.

Local Guesthouses
Local Homestays: Immerse yourself in Goan culture by choosing a local homestay, often run by hospitable residents.

Recommendations:
"Surya Kiran Heritage Hotel" in Panaji: Offers affordable rates and a glimpse into traditional Goan life. Website: www.hotelsuryakiran.com, Phone: +91-832-2427224.

"Casa Menezes" in Batim Village: Experience colonial charm in a heritage homestay. Website: www.casamenezesgoa.com, Phone: +91-832-2268088.

Budget Travel Tips
Advance Reservations: Secure your ideal budget stay by booking in advance, especially during peak tourist seasons.

Off-Peak Travel: Plan your trip during shoulder seasons to enjoy quieter surroundings and more favorable accommodation prices.

Negotiation Skills: Don't hesitate to negotiate prices, particularly for extended stays, as many budget accommodations are open to flexibility.

Shared Facilities: Be aware that some budget accommodations may offer shared bathrooms to keep costs lower. Confirm the amenities before booking.

Booking Websites

Utilize platforms such as Booking.com, Hostelworld, and Airbnb to explore a variety of budget accommodations tailored to your preferences.

In Goa, budget-friendly accommodations go beyond being a mere place to rest; they are your gateway to immersing yourself fully in the charm of this coastal gem. Whether it's a cozy guesthouse, a rustic beach hut, or an authentic homestay, these options allow you to maximize your experience of Goa's landscapes, culture, and memories.

Mid-range Accommodations

As you set foot in Goa, a myriad of accommodation options welcomes you, each designed to cater to a diverse range of budgets and preferences. For those seeking a balance between comfort and cost, Goa offers a plethora of mid-range accommodations that provide a step up in luxury without an overwhelming strain on your budget. Whether you're a couple seeking a romantic retreat, a family on vacation, or friends ready to explore, these mid-range options offer a delightful blend of convenience and value, ensuring your stay in Goa is both memorable and satisfying.

Boutique Hotels and Resorts

Boutique Hotels

Tucked away in scenic corners of Goa, boutique hotels provide a personalized and intimate experience. These establishments often boast unique architecture, stylish decor, and attentive service, creating an atmosphere of exclusivity.

Recommendations

"Acron Waterfront Resort" in Baga: Nestled by the Baga River, this boutique gem offers elegance and tranquility. Website: www.acronwaterfrontresortgoa.com, Phone: +91-832-2269600.

"The Postcard Cuelim" in Cuelim: Experience a blend of heritage and modern luxury in this charming boutique stay. Website: www.thepostcard.com, Phone: +91-832-2731930.

Resorts

Mid-range resorts in Goa often offer a comprehensive package of amenities, including swimming pools, on-site restaurants, and recreational activities. These resorts allow you to indulge in a luxurious experience without breaking the bank.

Recommendations

"Whispering Palms Beach Resort" in Candolim: A tranquil oasis with lush gardens and a relaxing atmosphere. Website: www.whisperingpalms.com, Phone: +91-832-6651515.

"Estrela Do Mar Beach Resort" in Calangute: Enjoy direct beach access and a range of facilities in this vibrant resort. Website: www.estreladomargoa.com, Phone: +91-832-2277375.

Heritage Stay and Guesthouses

Heritage Stay

Immerse yourself in Goa's rich history by opting for a heritage stay. These restored properties exude old-world charm while offering modern comforts.

Recommendations

"Panjim Inn" in Fontainhas: A historic mansion turned into a cozy heritage stay, capturing the essence of Goa's Portuguese influence. Website: www.panjiminn.com, Phone: +91-832-2226523.

"Siolim House" in Siolim: A 350-year-old heritage home offering a glimpse into Goa's colonial past. Website: www.siolimhouse.com, Phone: +91-832-2272138.

Upscale Guesthouses

Providing a blend of comfort and personalized service, upscale guesthouses offer an intimate experience without the formality of a hotel.

Recommendations

"Casa Tres Amigos" in Assagao: A luxurious guesthouse offering spacious rooms and a tranquil ambiance. Website: www.casatresamigosgoa.com, Phone: +91-982-258-2700.

"Villa Paradiso" in Anjuna: A charming Mediterranean-style guesthouse with a warm and inviting atmosphere. Website: www.villaparadisogoa.com, Phone: +91-982-248-7775.

Tips for Mid-range Travel

Book in Advance: Secure your mid-range accommodation ahead of time, especially during peak tourist seasons.

Amenities and Extras: Mid-range accommodations often include amenities such as swimming pools, spa facilities, and on-site dining. Take advantage of these extras.

Location Matters: Consider the proximity of your chosen accommodation to your preferred attractions, whether it's the beach, historical sites, or local markets.

In Goa, mid-range accommodations offer a harmonious blend of comfort, convenience, and affordability. Whether you opt for a boutique hotel, a resort with comprehensive amenities, a heritage stay, or an upscale guesthouse, these options let you enjoy Goa's beauty and charm without compromising on the quality of your stay.

Luxury Accommodations

As you step into Goa's enchanting landscape, a world of accommodation options unfolds before you, each catering to diverse budgets and preferences. For those seeking an exceptional level of comfort and indulgence, Goa presents an array of luxury accommodations that promise opulence and elegance beyond compare. Whether you're a couple in search of a romantic haven, a family celebrating a special occasion, or a traveler accustomed to the finest experiences, Goa's luxury accommodations offer an unparalleled gateway to an unforgettable sojourn.

Beachfront Resorts and Villas

Beachfront Resorts

Goa's luxurious beachfront resorts redefine lavish living with a blend of stunning ocean vistas, impeccable service, and state-of-the-art amenities. Experience a seamless fusion of natural beauty and modern sophistication.

Recommendations

"Alila Diwa Goa" in Majorda Beach: A serene retreat offering private access to the beach and exceptional spa facilities. Website: www.alilahotels.com, Phone: +91-832-2746800.

"The Leela Goa" in Mobor Beach: An iconic resort known for its world-class facilities, lush gardens, and private beach. Website: www.theleela.com, Phone: +91-832-6621234.

Private Villas

Indulge in the ultimate luxury by renting a private villa that offers seclusion, personalized service, and a home away from home. These villas often feature exclusive pools, lush gardens, and spacious interiors.

Recommendations

"Villa Morjim" in Morjim: A stunning beachfront villa with contemporary design and panoramic ocean views. Website: www.villamorjim.com, Phone: +91-982-112-9914.

"Villa Calangute" in Calangute: A luxurious villa with modern amenities, perfect for a group getaway. Website: www.villacalangute.com, Phone: +91-982-112-9914.

Heritage Properties and Boutique Retreats

Heritage Properties: Immerse yourself in Goa's rich history by staying in a heritage property. These meticulously restored mansions offer a glimpse into the region's colonial past while providing a luxurious stay.

Recommendations

"Taj Fort Aguada Resort & Spa" in Sinquerim: A historic fortress turned into a luxury resort, offering breathtaking views of the Arabian Sea. Website: www.tajhotels.com, Phone: +91-832-6645858.

"Nilaya Hermitage" in Arpora: A boutique retreat nestled amidst lush surroundings, offering tranquility and exquisite design. Website: www.nilayahermitage.com, Phone: +91-982-281-0608.

Luxury Hotels and Suites

Luxury Hotels: Goa's luxury hotels provide impeccable service, elegant decor, and a range of amenities to cater to your every need. Enjoy the epitome of comfort and sophistication.

Recommendations:

"W Goa" in Vagator: A luxury hotel known for its contemporary design, vibrant ambiance, and beachfront location. Website: www.marriott.com, Phone: +91-832-6718888.

"Grand Hyatt Goa" in Bambolim: A grand resort offering world-class facilities, lush gardens, and stunning architecture. Website: www.hyatt.com, Phone: +91-832-3011234.

Luxury Travel Tips
Advance Reservations: Given the exclusivity of luxury accommodations, book well in advance to secure your preferred dates.

Personalized Experiences: Luxury accommodations often offer personalized services such as private butlers, spa treatments, and gourmet dining experiences.

Location Consideration: Choose a luxury accommodation that aligns with your desired experiences, whether it's beachfront views, historical charm, or serene seclusion.

In Goa, luxury accommodations transcend mere lodgings; they are gateways to an unparalleled realm of lavish living and unforgettable experiences. Whether it's a beachfront resort, a private villa, a heritage property, or a luxury hotel, these accommodations let you revel in the magnificence of Goa while being pampered in opulence.

Chapter 4: The Best Beaches in Goa

Anjuna Beach

Anjuna Beach, located on Goa's northern coast, is a symbol of both tranquility and vivacity, a location where the bohemian spirit of the past blends with the natural beauty of the present. Anjuna Beach, one of Goa's most popular and colorful beaches, has a rich history dating back to the hippie era of the 1960s. It is still a timeless paradise for tourists looking for a combination of relaxation, lively culture, and breathtaking landscapes.

Beach Vibe and Atmosphere
Anjuna Beach is well-known for its relaxed ambiance and carefree mood. The soft murmur of the waves and a calming coastal breeze meet you as you tread onto the golden sands. The beachfront is a blank canvas with a combination of local shacks, beach bars, and palm trees swaying to the beat of the sea. It's a gathering place for

travelers from all over the globe to share their tales, experiences, and humor.

Hippie Heritage and Sunset Drum Circles

Anjuna's history is intertwined with the hippie movement that thrived here in the 1960s and 1970s. The famed "Anjuna Flea Market," where colorful kiosks provide a kaleidoscope of handicrafts, jewelry, apparel, and art, continues to carry on the legacy of bygone times. Every Wednesday, the beach comes alive with the bright energy of the market, encouraging you to discover its treasures and immerse yourself in a one-of-a-kind shopping experience.

Another well-known tradition is the "Sunset Drum Circle." As the sun sets, residents and visitors congregate to beat drums and dance together, producing an amazing rhythm that resonates around the beach. It's an enthralling display that personifies the spirit of liberty, expression, and harmony.

Adventure and Water Sports

64

Anjuna Beach is a haven for adventure seekers in addition to being a place of relaxation. The beach provides a variety of water sports activities, from parasailing to jet skiing, that allow you to explore the turquoise waters and enjoy the excitement of the sea. Consider taking a leisurely walk down the coastline or indulging in a yoga session against the background of the rising sun if you're looking for more tranquil activities.

Nightlife and Dining Options Abound

The eating scene in Anjuna reflects its varied nature, with beach shacks and restaurants serving a wide range of food. You may sample a combination of flavors that appeal to all palates, from local Goan pleasures to worldwide sensations. As the sun goes down, the beach changes into a hotspot for nightlife. The beach shacks and bars come alive after dark with music, dancing, and lively discussions, encouraging you to feel the excitement of Goa.

Practical Tips

Visiting Time: Anjuna Beach is enjoyable year-round, but the peak season is from November to February when the weather is mild and conducive to beach activities.

Market Day: Visit on a Wednesday to witness the vibrant Anjuna Flea Market in all its vibrant grandeur.

Respect Local Culture: While Anjuna has a laid-back vibe, it's important to respect local customs and traditions.

Anjuna Beach embodies the spirit of Goa's diverse allure. The beach provides a diverse experience that connects with guests seeking authenticity and adventure, from its vivid history and cultural heritage to its tranquil beauty and bustling vitality. Anjuna Beach is an important stop on any Goa adventure, beckoning you to make your memories along its sun-kissed sands, whether you're attracted to its bohemian tradition or charmed by its coastal beauty.

Arambol Beach

Tucked away in Goa's northern reaches, Arambol Beach is a hidden treasure that flawlessly mixes natural beauty with a distinct and creative environment. Arambol is a place that appeals to those searching for a calm retreat as well as those wishing to embrace a feeling of community and expression. It is known for its tranquil coastlines, bohemian culture, and active arts scene.

Peaceful Atmosphere and Scenic Beauty
Arambol Beach welcomes you with its quiet and natural beauty. The silky, golden sands of the coastline invite you to relax and absorb up the sun's warm beams. Unlike other of Goa's busier beaches, Arambol retains a tranquil ambiance, making it a great option for people looking for a quiet getaway. The gentle waves and clean waters provide an attractive atmosphere for swimming and wading, making it ideal for both families and lone tourists.

Artistic Expression and Bohemian Culture

Arambol's bohemian and artistic vibe is what sets it distinct. The beach attracts musicians, artists, and free spirits from all over the globe, resulting in a mingling of cultures and influences. The beachfront is alive with creative energy, as visitors and residents gather to tell tales, make music, and participate in open-air jam sessions. The feeling of community is obvious, and the open-minded atmosphere supports all types of self-expression.

Sunsets & Drum Circles

Arambol Beach is noted for its spectacular sunset drum circles, an event that exemplifies the beach's feeling of oneness and creativity. As the sun sets, people assemble to make rhythm and music with different instruments ranging from drums to tambourines. This spontaneous gathering is a sight to see, representing Arambol's free-spirited ethos.

Holistic Wellness and Yoga

Arambol, in addition to its creative atmosphere, provides a place for healing and self-discovery. The beach is a refuge for yoga practitioners, with courses that enable you to balance your body, mind, and soul against the tranquil Arabian Sea background. Holistic activities such as meditation and reiki are also prevalent, allowing a chance to revitalize and harmonize your inner self.

Organic Delights and Local Markets

The creative flare of Arambol extends to the local markets, where you may buy a variety of unique crafts, apparel, jewelry, and curiosities. The markets highlight the abilities of local artists and provide a venue for the community's creative expressions. Arambol also has various organic cafés and restaurants where you may experience nutritious and nutritional treats while watching the serene sea.

Practical Tips

Seasonal Visit: The greatest time to visit Arambol Beach is during the dry season, which runs from November to March and is ideal for outdoor activities.

Sun Protection: Remember to apply sunscreen and stay hydrated, especially during the peak sun hours.

Music & Nightlife: Immerse yourself in Arambol's dynamic music scene by attending one of the numerous live music sessions or taking part in a sunset drum circle.

Arambol Beach is a destination for individuals looking for peace & quiet, creative inspiration, and a dynamic feeling of community. Arambol provides an entire experience that connects with the soul, whether you're attracted to the quiet shoreline, the creativity in the air, or the unique combination of holistic health. It's a location where the cadence of the waves reflects the rhythm of self-expression, allowing you to embrace the present and create memories that are inextricably linked to the spirit of this enthralling destination.

Vagator Beach

Vagator Beach, located on Goa's northern coast, is a stunning canvas that perfectly mixes natural grandeur with a free-spirited ambiance. Vagator is a place that provides a harmonic blend of tranquility and excitement, making it a favorite among both sunseekers and those wishing to experience Goa's creative pulse. It is known for its breathtaking cliffs, active nightlife, and compelling energy.

Panoramic Views and Cliffs

Vagator Beach is distinguished by its spectacular red cliffs that overlook the Arabian Sea's blue waters. These cliffs not only give spectacular panoramic vistas but also add to the beach's distinct character. The sharp contrast between the reddish-brown cliffs and the deep blue sea produces a beautiful visual spectacle.

Two Sides of Vagator

Vagator Beach is often split into two sections: Big Vagator and Little Vagator. Big Vagator, also known as North Vagator, has a lively environment with shacks, restaurants, and beach clubs. This region is popular with visitors looking for beachside relaxation, excellent food, and lively nightlife.

Little Vagator, also known as Ozran Beach, on the other hand, radiates a more relaxed and quiet attitude. This section is tucked behind the cliffs and provides a calmer hideaway where you may relax surrounded by natural beauty, with a feeling of isolation that inspires introspection.

Chapora Fort and Heritage

The magnificent Chapora Fort is perched above the cliffs overlooking Vagator Beach. This ancient fort, which dates back to the 17th century, not only provides an insight into Goa's colonial history but also provides panoramic views of the coastline. The hike up to the fort is an adventure in and of itself, bringing you through lush foliage before rewarding you with stunning views that spread as far as the eye can see.

Vivacious Nightlife and Sunset Vibes

As the sun sets, Vagator Beach comes alive, and the beachfront morphs into a hotspot of lively nightlife. Beach shacks, bars, and clubs are illuminated, encouraging you to dance, interact, and enjoy the strong Goan spirit. Vagator has a variety of entertainment choices to suit all interests, ranging from live music performances to exciting DJ sets.

Vagator's Bohemian Essence

Bohemian culture is strongly ingrained in the spirit of Vagator. The beach's creative energy attracts artists, musicians, and free spirits from all over the globe, resulting in a varied and open-minded environment. This is evident not just in the area's busy nightlife, but also in the markets, art exhibits, and cultural events.

Practical Tips

Visiting Time: Vagator Beach is delightful all year, although the main tourist season runs from February to November when the weather is good and suited to outdoor activities.

Visit Chapora Fort: If you're in Vagator, don't miss out on exploring Chapora Fort and photographing the spectacular sunset views.

Swimming Safety: when the waters may look calm, be mindful of different currents and depths when swimming.

Vagator Beach is an enthralling combination of natural beauty, lively culture, and enthralling energy. Vagator encourages you to experience both its tranquil and thrilling sides, whether you're attracted to its breathtaking cliffs, busy nightlife, or the bohemian vibe that pervades the environment. It's a spot where the thundering waves blend with the sounds of the night, where spectacular landscapes meet the free-spirited character of Goa, resulting in an experience that's as compelling as it is memorable.

Morjim Beach

Morjim Beach, located on Goa's calm northern coast, is a refuge of serenity and natural beauty, gaining the nickname "Turtle Beach" owing to its importance as a breeding location for endangered sea turtles. Morjim is a place that allows people to repose to pristine surroundings and absorb the calming rhythm of the sea. It is known for its untouched coastlines, moderate waves, and relaxing ambiance.

Soft Sands and Pristine Shores

Morjim Beach is a long length of smooth golden sands that reach as far as the eye can see. The calm ambiance of the beach is ideal for people looking for a peaceful vacation from the hustle and bustle of daily life. The calm waves wash at your feet as you walk down the beach, producing a relaxing song that connects with your spirit.

The Conservation of Turtles and Their Ecological Importance

Morjim Beach's importance as a breeding location for Olive Ridley sea turtles is one of its most notable features. Between November and March, these endangered animals visit the seashore to lay their eggs, producing a natural display that grabs the hearts of nature lovers and environmentalists alike. Efforts to conserve and maintain these turtles have resulted in Morjim being designated as a conservation zone, emphasizing the fragile ecological balance that this beach sustains.

Quiet Ambiance and Relaxation

Morjim's ambiance is characterized by its calmness and lack of busy throng. Unlike other of Goa's busier beaches, Morjim provides a tranquil hideaway where you can relax and take in the scenery. The beach's laid-back ambiance attracts visitors looking for peace and a feeling of connection with nature.

Birdwatching Paradise

Morjim is recognized as a birdwatcher's paradise, in addition to its immaculate sands and crystal-clear waters. The beach's closeness to the Chapora River, as well as its marshy environs, provide a perfect home for a wide variety of bird species. Morjim is a birdwatching heaven, with migrating birds as well as local species, allowing a chance to observe nature's magnificence in action.

Yoga and Holistic Retreats

Morjim's calm ambiance is ideal for yoga and holistic health activities. Many nearby resorts and retreat facilities offer yoga lessons, meditation sessions, and wellness programs that enable you to restore your mind, body, and soul against the beautiful Arabian Sea background.

Practical Tips

Turtle Nesting Season: If you want to see the nesting activity of Olive Ridley sea turtles, go between November and March.

Sun Protection: Apply sunscreen and wear proper protective clothing, particularly during high sun hours.

Responsible Tourism: Given Morjim's ecological significance, be sure to follow guidelines to protect the nesting turtles and their habitat.

Morjim Beach is a haven of peace and natural beauty, encouraging visitors to see Goa's coastline in its purest form. Morjim provides an experience that connects with the rhythm of nature, whether you're attracted by the nesting sea turtles, lured to the tranquil shoreline, or seeking a calm getaway. It's a spot where the sands retain life's mysteries and the waves whisper conservation stories, resulting in an experience that will leave you both revitalized and inspired.

Palolem Beach

Palolem Beach, located on Goa's southern coast, is a calm retreat that encapsulates the spirit of a serene tropical paradise. Palolem has earned its spot as one of Goa's most picturesque and sought-after attractions due to its crescent-shaped shoreline, pure blue waters, and easygoing environment. Palolem's appeal is likely to grab your heart, whether you're looking for a calm escape or a mix of leisure and adventure.

Swaying Palms and Crescent Bay
The beauty of Palolem is defined by its beautiful crescent-shaped bay, where soft waves wash against the

shoreline in a harmonic dance. The beach is lined with swaying coconut trees, which give shelter and a tranquil background while you soak up the sun's rays.

Relaxed Atmosphere and Unwinding

One of Palolem's distinguishing features is its relaxed and unpretentious attitude. Unlike several of Goa's busier beaches, Palolem promotes leisure and a slower pace of life. The beach's quiet environment is enhanced by the lack of huge crowds and commercial constructions, making it a great spot to rest and revitalize.

Nighttime Magic and Silent Noise Parties

Palolem's nightlife is distinct and intriguing, with "Silent Noise" parties gaining popularity over time. Wearing headphones and dancing to music delivered via them creates a weird and immersive experience at these parties. As night sets, the beachfront comes alive with the illumination of lanterns and the sound of laughing, encouraging you to discover Palolem's enchanting charm after dark.

Water and Land Adventures

While Palolem values calm, it also provides a variety of water and land-based activities for those seeking adventure. From kayaking across the tranquil waters to visiting surrounding islands and secret coves, the beach offers a distinct viewpoint on Goa's natural beauty. In addition, the adjacent Cotigao Wildlife Sanctuary provides trekking options through beautiful forests as well as the opportunity to see a variety of flora and wildlife.

Charming Shacks and Delectable Cuisine

Palolem's beachfront is lined with lovely shacks and beachfront restaurants. These restaurants provide a broad gastronomic environment, ranging from traditional Goan fare to international fare. A seafood feast beneath the open sky, accompanied by rhythmic waves, is an integral aspect of the Palolem experience.

Practical Tips

Ideal Time to Visit: The dry season, from November to March, is the greatest time to visit Palolem Beach since the weather is nice and suited to outdoor activities.

Beach Essentials: Remember to pack essentials such as sunscreen, a hat, sunglasses, and a beach towel to ensure a comfortable day at the beach.

Responsible Tourism: Help maintain Palolem's natural beauty by practicing responsible tourism, such as carrying reusable items and avoiding littering.

Palolem Beach exemplifies the calm and natural beauty that Goa is known for. Palolem welcomes you to enjoy a bit of paradise on the southern shoreline, whether you're attracted to its stunning bay, tranquil environment, or distinctive nightlife activities. It's a location where the sands whisper secrets of adventure and the spirit of Goa's coastal beauty comes to life with every gentle swing of the palms.

Calangute Beach

Calangute Beach, located on Goa's northern coast, has the famous title of "Queen of Beaches." Calangute Beach is a lively location that caters to a varied variety of people. It is known for its dynamic atmosphere, large shoreline, and a myriad of activities. This popular beach provides a variety of activities that encapsulate the essence of Goa's coastal charm, from water sports aficionados to shopaholics and beach lovers.

Sun, Sea, and Sand

Calangute's allure stems from its vast length of golden sands that stretches along the Arabian Sea. The gentle sands are ideal for sunbathing, beach volleyball, or strolls along the water's edge. The beach changes into a magnificent backdrop when the sun sets, enticing you to watch the sky blazing with orange and pink colors.

Water Sports Extravaganza

Calangute Beach is a paradise of water sports activities for people looking for an adrenaline rush. From paragliding and jet skiing to banana boat rides and bumper boat experiences, the beach has a variety of activities to satisfy your need for action. Professional operators assure your safety while providing a thrilling element to your beach experience.

Shopping and Local Flavors

Calangute's lively streets are dotted with a variety of stores and booths, making it a shopping paradise. From contemporary apparel to souvenirs and handicrafts, there is a wide variety of things to satisfy all preferences. The lively Calangute Market is a center for both local and international items, allowing you to take a bit of Goa home with you.

Entertainment and Nightlife

Calangute's nightlife comes to life as the sun sets below the horizon. Live music, DJ sets, and dance floors entice you to sway to the sounds of Goa's pulsating nightlife at beach shacks and adjacent clubs. It's an opportunity to immerse oneself in the lively atmosphere and make memories that reflect the region's carefree character.

Dining Delights

Calangute has a diverse food scene that appeals to a wide range of tastes. The beachfront restaurants and shacks provide a broad menu that will satisfy your appetites, ranging from traditional Goan meals to international cuisine. A seafood feast with a view of the sea is an integral aspect of the Calangute experience.

Practical Tips

Peak Season Crowding: Keep in mind that Calangute may get busy during the peak tourist season (November to February). Arrive early to grab a decent beach location.

Water Safety: When participating in water sports, emphasize safety by following the directions of qualified operators.

Sun Protection: Apply sunscreen, wear a hat, and remain hydrated to protect yourself from the sun.

Calangute Beach's lively attitude and diverse offers make it a must-see for tourists seeking a mix of leisure, adventure, and colorful experiences. Calangute reflects the spirit of Goa's coastal variety, whether you're enthralled by the water sports, delighted by the retail scene, or attracted by the throbbing nightlife. It's a location where the sands tell stories of adventure, the waves reveal secrets of leisure, and the heart of Goa's beach culture pulses in time with the rhythms of the sea.

Baga Beach

Baga Beach, located between Calangute and Anjuna, is a bustling playground for people looking for a mix of action and tranquility. Baga Beach attracts visitors looking for an action-packed coastal retreat due to its active ambiance, abundance of water sports, and vibrant nightlife scene.

Haven for Water Sports
Baga's coastlines are famous for spectacular water sports for adventurers of all levels. The beach provides a wealth

of alternatives for making a splash and creating amazing experiences, from jet skiing and parasailing to banana boat rides and windsurfing. While you enjoy the adrenaline thrill, professional instructors safeguard your safety.

Beach Shacks and Gourmet Delights

Baga Beach is peppered with quaint beach shacks and restaurants that urge you to go on a gastronomic adventure. While enjoying the sea breeze, indulge in Goan specialties, seafood delicacies, and international cuisines. At night, the beach shacks morph into exciting centers, with live music, DJ sets, and the opportunity to dance beneath the stars.

Nightlife Extravaganza

Baga's nightlife is famed and alluring. Tito's Avenue, a busy avenue dotted with clubs and bars, attracts revelers from all over the globe. Live music, electronic rhythms, and themed parties illuminate the night, creating an electrifying environment that is typical of Goa's lively nightlife.

Shopping and Local Discoveries

Baga's streets are a shopper's paradise, with a plethora of boutiques and kiosks selling apparel, accessories, souvenirs, and other items. The Saturday Night Market at Baga is a must-see for its unusual mix of local crafts, international items, and colorful carnival atmosphere.

Practical Tips

Peak Season Crowds: During peak season, Baga Beach may get busy. Arrive early in the day to get a comfy beach location.

Water Safety: Prioritize your safety when participating in water sports by following the recommendations issued by approved operators.

Baga's popularity implies that traffic might be congested during peak hours. Consider adopting other modes of transportation, such as scooters or walking, to get about the region.

Baga Beach's vibrant attitude and variety of activities make it a popular choice for anyone looking for a fun beach experience. Baga offers a journey that connects with the lively core of Goa's coastal culture, whether you're attracted to water sports, fascinated by the nightlife, or interested in the retail scene. It's a location where the waves of excitement meet the beaches of tranquility, resulting in an atmosphere that's as energizing as it is captivating.

Agonda Beach

Agonda Beach, located in South Goa, has a distinct appeal when contrasted to the busier beaches farther north. Agonda, known for its quiet ambiance, is a haven for those seeking a relaxing respite among nature's splendor. Its leisurely pace and pristine scenery make it a popular location for those seeking tranquility and a connection with the coastal environment.

Secluded Sands and Untouched Beauty

The unspoiled shoreline of Agonda extends elegantly, providing a feeling of space and seclusion that is uncommon on many of Goa's busier beaches. The silky sands urge you to unwind and rest beneath the soothing shade of swaying palms, while the tranquil waves offer the ideal soundtrack for peaceful reflection.

Haven for Yoga and Wellness

With various yoga retreats and health institutes dotting the region, Agonda's peacefulness makes it a great backdrop for wellness activities. Joining a yoga class to reconnect with your inner self, meditating by the sea, or indulging in revitalizing spa treatments that merge effortlessly with the calming sounds of the ocean are all options.

A Village Vibe that Meanders

With its laid-back attitude and a handful of restaurants and cafes serving both local and international cuisines, the town that borders Agonda Beach is equally attractive. The pace of life on the beach is leisurely and easygoing, establishing a natural balance between land and water.

Turtle Nesting Sanctuary

The coasts of Agonda also serve as breeding grounds for Olive Ridley turtles. During nesting season, you get the unique chance to observe these gorgeous birds depositing their eggs on the sands. Responsible tourist activities safeguard the safety of these threatened animals and their habitats.

Practical Tips

Relaxation and reflection: Agonda Beach is great for people looking for peace. Accept the pace of the place and utilize this time to recharge and reflect.

Responsible Tourism: If you encounter nesting turtles, maintain a respectful distance and avoid using flash photography, as it can distress the turtles.

Light Footprint: Respect the pristine environment by leaving no trace. Take your rubbish with you and be careful of your environmental effects.

Agonda Beach exemplifies the serene and pristine beauty that Goa's coastline has to offer. Agonda invites you to enjoy a calmer, more contemplative side of the coastal experience, whether you're attracted to its isolated shoreline, interested in the yoga and health facilities, or charmed by the opportunity to see turtle nesting. It's a location where the waves whisper stories of tranquility, the sands hide natural wonders, and the soul finds consolation in nature's soft embrace.

Chapter 5: Attractions Beyond the Beaches

Exploring the Historic Charm of Old Goa

Beyond the sun-kissed beaches and the rhythmic waves, Old Goa is a treasure mine of history and heritage, providing a look into the region's illustrious past. Old Goa, also known as Velha Goa, was once the capital of Portuguese India and is a living witness to the region's blend of cultures, religions, and architectural wonders. You'll be taken back in time as you walk through its old streets and majestic cathedrals, to an age of grandeur and importance.

A Look at Goa's Colonial Legacy

During the 16th and 17th centuries, Old Goa was the core of Portuguese imperial power in Asia. This era's relics are engraved into the terrain in the form of majestic buildings that represent the art, culture, and faith of the period. The city was once dubbed the "Lisbon of the East," and the architecture that graces its streets bears witness to its greatness.

Basilica of Bom Jesus: A Sacred Relic

The Basilica of Bom Jesus is a treasured landmark in Old Goa. The mortal remains of St. Francis Xavier, a venerated figure in Christian history, are housed in this UNESCO World Heritage Site. With its complex features and magnificent façade, the basilica's baroque architecture is a pleasure to see. Inside, the marble floor shows events from St. Francis Xavier's life, enabling visitors to reflect on his legacy.

Se Cathedral: A Marvel of Faith and Architecture

The Se Cathedral, another amazing monument that dominates Old Goa, stands as an icon of Goa's dedication and architectural talent. This cathedral, dedicated to St. Catherine, is Asia's biggest and has an awe-inspiring combination of Portuguese-Manueline and Tuscan architectural styles. Its golden bell, known as the

"Golden Bell of Goa," connects with history and still rings today.

St. Augustine Tower: Ancient Monastery Relics

The imposing ruins of St. Augustine's Church and Convent evoke memories of a once-thriving Augustinian monastery. The lone remaining building is the huge St. Augustine Tower, which offers panoramic views of Old Goa from its heights. The tale of this complex's growth and demise lends fascination to the experience of seeing these magnificent remains.

Archaeological Museum: Unveiling the Past

The Archaeological Museum offers a selected collection of artifacts that give insights into the region's rich past for those who want to go even further into the history of Old Goa. The museum's displays, which range from sculptures and paintings to historical artifacts, bridge the gap between the past and the present, enabling visitors to appreciate the rich heritage that Old Goa symbolizes.

Practical Tips

Appropriate Attire: Because many of the attractions in Old Goa are religious, it is best to dress modestly, with shoulders and knees covered.

Exploration Time: Allocate at least half a day to explore the key attractions in Old Goa. Some facilities, such as the Archaeological Museum, may have limited hours of operation.

The ancient appeal of Old Goa is reflected in its painstakingly maintained monuments and memories of a bygone age. Every stride through its historic streets offers another layer of history, culture, and spirituality. You're not simply experiencing the past when you visit its churches, ruins, and museums; you're also taking part in a trip that honors the tremendous imprint of the Portuguese colonial legacy on the vivid canvas of Goa's history.

Temples and Churches

Goa's spiritual tapestry is intertwined with a rich weave of temples and churches that stand as timeless icons of faith, culture, and history beyond the sun-drenched coastlines and busy streets. This eclectic mix of religious architecture represents the region's peaceful coexistence of religions and provides tourists with a one-of-a-kind chance to experience the spiritual essence that determines Goa's character.

Temples
The temples of Goa provide witness to the deep spiritual beliefs that have flourished here for millennia. The beautiful buildings that dot the state's landscapes represent the state's Hindu heritage.

Shri Mangeshi Temple: A Spiritual Oasis
The Shri Mangeshi Temple is a major Hindu temple in Ponda that commemorates Lord Mangesh, a manifestation of Lord Shiva. The architectural beauty

and tranquil environs of the temple make it a sanctuary for both spiritual seekers and architecture aficionados.

Shanta Durga Temple: A Peaceful Place of Devotion
This temple, dedicated to Goddess Shantadurga, displays Goa's religious heritage's unique combination of Indian and Portuguese elements. Its peaceful atmosphere and lively events make it an important element of the state's cultural mosaic.

Churches
The existence of exquisite churches attests to the Portuguese colonial rule's ongoing impact in Goa. These architectural wonders stand watch over history, each telling a different narrative from the region's past.

Basilica of Bom Jesus: A Spiritual Landmark
This UNESCO World Heritage Site combines Baroque architecture with spiritual importance. The basilica's solemnity, which houses the bones of St. Francis Xavier, inspires visitors to contemplate the interweaving of faith and history.

The Se Cathedral: A Symbol of Faith

The Se Cathedral, with its grandeur and historical importance, is a testament to Goa's devotion. The opulent interiors and towering facade pay tribute to the legacy of faith that impacted the history of the state.

Chapel of St. Catherine: Simplicity in Splendor

The Chapel of St. Catherine, perched on a hillside, provides beautiful views of the surrounding area. The chapel's simplicity and historical significance give a peaceful environment for reflection.

Practical Tips

Respectful Attire: It is suggested to dress modestly while visiting temples and churches, covering shoulders and knees as a gesture of respect.

Cultural Sensitivity: Keep in mind that places of worship hold deep spiritual significance. Maintain a courteous approach and refrain from interfering with existing rites.

Goa's temples and churches are live reminders of the region's rich spiritual and cultural heritage. When you enter these hallowed sites, you are not only beginning an exploratory voyage, but you are also interacting with the threads that weave Goa's varied tapestry. These temples and churches encourage you to immerse yourself in the spiritual legacy that continues to influence the state's character, whether you're intrigued by the complex architecture, pulled by the spiritual resonance, or seeking a better knowledge of Goa's history.

Goa's Museums and Art Galleries

Beyond the sun-kissed beachfront and bustling streets, museums and art galleries preserve and commemorate Goa's cultural history. These cultural institutions provide an intriguing look into the region's history, creative expression, and the interplay of many influences that have defined Goa's character.

A Journey Through Time at the Goa State Museum

The Goa State Museum, located in the center of Panaji, is a treasure trove of artifacts from diverse eras of history. Its collection contains sculptures, coins, manuscripts, and artworks that illuminate Goa's history and unique tapestry of cultures.

The Archaeological Section displays old sculptures, ceramics, and artifacts that depict the state's historical progression from the prehistoric to the colonial period.

The art gallery inside the museum has a collection of paintings and modern artworks that showcase the creative talent that flourishes in Goa.

Christian Art area: This area exhibits religious artifacts, paintings, and sculptures that give testament to the region's colonial history, providing insights into Goa's Christian heritage.

Goa Chitra Museum: A Glimpse into Tradition
The Goa Chitra Museum, located in Benaulim, is a tribute to the state's rural history. The ethnographic

artifacts, tools, and implements on display at the museum provide a glimpse into Goa's agrarian heritage and traditional way of life.

Cultural Diversity: Exhibits at the museum examine the many populations that have contributed to Goa's cultural mosaic, providing an understanding of the region's complex tapestry of traditions and practices.

Sculpture Garden: The sculpture garden of the Goa Chitra Museum is an outdoor environment decorated with traditional Goan sculptures, giving an immersive experience that takes visitors to the bygone ages.

Pilar Museum: A Spiritual Archive
Situated in Pilar, the Pilar Museum is a place of spiritual and historical significance. It has a collection of religious artifacts, paintings, and sculptures that provide light on Christianity's great effect on Goa's heritage.

The displays of the Missionary Legacy Museum tell the stories of Christian missionaries who played an important part in Goa's history and cultural evolution.

Spiritual Art: The museum exhibits a variety of Christian art forms, including paintings, sculptures, and holy relics, that represent the region's strong faith.

Practical Tips
Opening Hours: Museum hours vary, so it's best to double-check before organizing a trip.

Respectful Conduct: When visiting museums and galleries, maintain a respectful demeanor and avoid touching or disturbing the exhibits.

The museums and art galleries in Goa provide a glimpse into the region's culture, history, and creative expression. Exploring these cultural havens takes you on a trip through time, showing the different influences that have contributed to Goa's distinct personality. Whether you're drawn to ancient artifacts, charmed by modern artworks, or interested in Goa's historical storylines, these museums and galleries allow you to immerse yourself in the rich tapestry of experiences that constitute the cultural canvas of Goa.

Wildlife Sanctuaries and Reserves

Goa's natural beauty goes beyond its sun-kissed beaches and lively streets to its pristine wildlife sanctuaries and reserves. These protected areas provide a look into the region's different ecosystems while also protecting rare and endangered animals. Goa's wildlife reserves, from lush forests to tranquil wetlands, provide a chance to interact with nature and see the mesmerizing cycle of life in its purest form.

Bhagwan Mahavir Wildlife Sanctuary: A Verdant Haven Situated in the Western Ghats, the Bhagwan Mahavir Wildlife Sanctuary is a sanctuary for nature enthusiasts and wildlife lovers. Its lush forests, glistening waterfalls, and winding trails provide a great habitat for a wide range of animals.

Dudhsagar Waterfalls: A highlight within the sanctuary, the Dudhsagar Waterfalls cascade down rock faces, creating a mesmerizing spectacle of foaming white waters against the backdrop of lush greenery.

Wildlife Diversity: The sanctuary is home to a wide variety of wildlife, including the Indian gaur, sambar deer, spotted deer, and various bird and butterfly species.

Cotigao Wildlife Sanctuary: A Green Retreat
The Cotigao Wildlife Sanctuary, located in South Goa, entices visitors with its serene ambiance and diverse biodiversity. Its lush canopy and moderate terrain make it an accessible nature getaway.

Treetop Watchtowers: Cotigao Sanctuary has high watchtowers that provide an immersive wildlife experience by allowing you to see the flora and animals from a unique vantage point.

Wildlife Encounters: Explore the sanctuary's trails to see local animals such as the Indian pangolin, flying squirrel, and different bird species in their natural habitat.

Bondla Wildlife Sanctuary: A Fun Family Adventure

The Bondla Wildlife Sanctuary is ideal for families and nature lovers since it combines educational opportunities with interactions with local creatures.

Mini Zoo: The refuge has a mini zoo where visitors may get up close and personal with animals such as sloth bears, monkeys, and deer.

Botanical Gardens: Bondla Sanctuary has botanical gardens where you may learn about various plant types endemic to the area.

Practical Tips
Nature-Friendly Attire: For your sanctuary trips, dress comfortably and wear sturdy shoes. Avoid using strong colors that may frighten the animals.

Guided Tours: Many wildlife sanctuaries provide guided tours that give in-depth information on the area's ecosystems, fauna, and conservation activities.

Goa's wildlife reserves and sanctuaries provide a revitalizing getaway into the heart of nature's bounty. When you visit these protected places, you are not only observing the region's biodiversity but also helping to conserve it. These sanctuaries urge you to disconnect from the world of man-made buildings and immerse yourself in the symphony of nature's rhythms, whether you're attracted to the rustling forests, the hypnotic waterfalls, or the possibility of meeting unusual species.

Chapter 6: Adventure and Outdoor Pursuits

Water Sports and Oceanic Thrills

Beyond the sun-kissed beaches, Goa's turquoise waters offer water lovers a world of adventure and excitement. The dynamic aquatic landscape of the coastline provides a playground for water activities ranging from the exciting to the calm, appealing to both adrenaline seekers and those seeking a more leisurely experience. Whether you're flying above the waves or diving to the bottom, Goa's water sports scene guarantees an unparalleled marine adventure.

Jet Skiing: Riding the Waves
Jet skiing is an exciting way to speed over the water's surface while experiencing the surge of wind and spray on your skin. You may safely ride the waves and enjoy the excitement of operating your watercraft with instructors on hand to help novices.

Parasailing: Soaring Above the Coastline

Enjoy a bird's-eye view of Goa's stunning coastline as you're gently hoisted into the sky and attached to a colorful parachute. The sense of weightlessness, along with the panoramic vistas, creates a fantastic experience that combines adventure and tranquility.

Windsurfing: Riding Wind and Waves

Windsurfing combines the skill of sailing with the exhilaration of surfing. You glide over the water's surface on a board while manipulating the sail to manage the waves by harnessing the strength of the wind. It's an excellent sport for individuals looking for a combination of ability and excitement.

Kayaking: Paddling Along Hidden Coves

Kayaking is a more leisurely water adventure that allows you to explore Goa's secret coves, mangroves, and estuaries. Glide across tranquil waters, surrounded by rich greenery and nature's calming sounds.

Snorkeling: Below the Water's Surface

Snorkeling in Goa's beautiful waters allows you to discover the underwater beauties of the state. Witness thriving marine life, vivid coral reefs, and the fascinating world under the waves. Snorkeling excursions are often accompanied by guides who maintain safety and give information about the marine habitat.

Scuba Diving: Exploring the Depths

Scuba diving provides an intimate experience of Goa's underwater realm, revealing a world of colorful marine life and hidden landscapes. You may go on guided dives with trained dive operators to explore coral gardens, shipwrecks, and aquatic species that live in the ocean.

Practical Tips

Safety First: Put your safety first by following the instructions of trained instructors and operators. Wear protective equipment and pay strict attention to instructions.

Responsible Practices: Choose operators who prioritize responsible and sustainable tourism practices, minimizing the impact on marine life and ecosystems.

The water sports scene in Goa beckons you to go beyond the beach and experience the limitless delights of the ocean. Each water sport provides a distinct view of Goa's magnificent coastline, whether you're flying above the waves, gliding with the breeze, or diving into the depths. As you immerse yourself in these oceanic thrills, you will find a world where adventure meets tranquility, and the beat of the waves will serve as a background to the memories you will make in Goa's aquatic playground.

Trekking and Hiking through Goa's Terrain

Goa's varied and interesting landscapes reveal a new dimension of its beauty beyond its sun-kissed beaches and colorful streets. Trekking and trekking in Goa provide an exceptional chance to discover the region's lush hinterlands, deep forests, and rolling hills. Whether

110

you're an enthusiastic trekker looking for new challenges or a nature lover looking for peace, Goa's terrain guarantees a remarkable voyage of discovery.

Trekking Trails for Everyone
The trails in Goa accommodate a broad variety of trekking skills, from easy hikes to strenuous treks requiring endurance and dedication.

Dudhsagar Waterfall Trek: A Majestic Trail
Begin your journey through the Bhagwan Mahavir Wildlife Sanctuary with the famed Dudhsagar Waterfall trek. The walk provides not only the delight of seeing the beautiful waterfall but also the excitement of crossing varied terrain.

Tambdi Surla Waterfall Trek: An Undiscovered Treasure
The Tambdi Surla Waterfall trek offers a more personal trekking experience, taking you through lush forests and lovely hamlets. The cascading waterfall is a peaceful haven in the middle of the wilderness.

Netravali Wildlife Sanctuary Trek: Verdant Exploration
Explore the Netravali Wildlife Sanctuary, where several hiking routes reveal the sanctuary's diverse biodiversity. Explore forests, streams, and fields while immersed in nature's embrace.

Sahyadri Range Treks: For the Avid Adventurer

Experienced hikers can scale the peaks of the Sahyadri Range, which runs along Goa's eastern border. These treks provide panoramic views of Goa's landscapes, highlighting the state's rough beauty.

Practical Tips
Guided Treks: Choose guided treks if you are unfamiliar with the terrain. Local guides give information about the trails' ecology, animals, and cultural value.

Appropriate Gear: Wear comfortable hiking shoes, light clothing, and carry essentials like water, snacks, and a first aid kit.

Trekking and trekking in Goa provides a unique opportunity to appreciate the region's natural splendor. As you travel across various landscapes, you will come into contact with the core of Goa's wilderness. Whether you're drawn to the rush of waterfalls, fascinated by the flora and animals, or just looking for peace in nature, these trails invite you to go on an adventure that goes beyond the usual. Accept the obstacles, absorb the vistas, and allow Goa's terrain to lead you on a journey of discovery and adventure.

Cycling Adventures: Exploring Off the Beaten Path

Goa provides a fantastic avenue for adventure on two wheels beyond the busy streets and prominent tourist destinations. Cycling trips allow you to immerse yourself in the region's tranquil landscapes, small villages, and secret nooks. Whether you're an enthusiastic cyclist looking for an adrenaline rush or a leisure rider looking for peaceful exploration, Goa's cycling trails offer a voyage of discovery via less-traveled routes.

113

A Cyclist's Haven

The varied terrain of Goa provides cycling trails to suit a wide variety of tastes and ability levels, offering an adventure for every sort of cyclist.

Backroads of Divar Island: A Tranquil Escape

Enjoy the beauty of Divar Island while cycling through its calm backroads. Discover old churches, verdant paddy fields, and traditional Goan residences while taking in the island's tranquil atmosphere.

Countryside Trails: Rural Delights

Explore Goa's rural interior, where bike trails weave through lovely villages. Travel across the countryside, via green farms, flowing rivers, and friendly residents.

Coastal Drives: Enjoying the Sea Breeze

Cycling along the magnificent coastline is a relaxing experience, with sea breezes and panoramic ocean vistas.

Explore secluded coves, fishing villages, and the Arabian Sea's ever-changing colors.

Western Ghats Escapades: For the Adventurous

The Western Ghats provide rugged terrain that offers an amazing cycling experience for anyone looking for a more demanding adventure. Conquer steep ascents, manage twisting descents, and be rewarded with beautiful vistas.

Practical Tips

Bicycle Rental: Many stores in tourist locations hire bicycles. Select a reputable rental provider that offers well-maintained bicycles and safety equipment.

Safety First: Wear a helmet, comfortable clothing, and appropriate footwear. Keep hydrated, have a map, and notify someone of your planned path.

Cycling activities in Goa entice you to explore at a slower pace. Whether you're biking through peaceful villages, coasting along stunning beaches, or tackling difficult hills, each ride provides a unique connection with the region's landscape and culture. Off the main route, you'll uncover Goa's hidden jewels, creating memories of discovery and immersion that go beyond the typical tourist experience. So, jump on a bicycle, feel the breeze on your skin, and let Goa's breathtaking splendor spread before your eyes as you begin on a cycling adventure of a lifetime.

Chapter 7: Nightlife and Entertainment

Navigating Goa's Vibrant Nightlife

As the sun sets over the Arabian Sea, Goa transforms into a wonderful paradise for night owls seeking exuberant entertainment. After nightfall, the coastal paradise comes alive with a throbbing energy that echoes through its beach shacks, clubs, live music venues, and lively parties. Navigating Goa's nightlife is like entering a realm where the music is infectious, the lights are hypnotic, and the celebrations never cease.

The Nightlife Spectrum from Sunset to Sunrise

Shoreside Vibes and Beach Shacks
As twilight falls, beach shacks along famous beaches such as Anjuna, Baga, and Calangute prepare for an evening of fun. As the waves sing the coast, sink into bean bags, drink cocktails, and dance to the beat of live

music. These shacks, which provide a mix of music, dancing, and seaside ambiance, are a must-see for a laid-back but lively night out.

Electronic Music Scene and Clubbing

Goa's famed clubs cater to all-night revelers who want thrilling tunes and dance floors that throb with energy. Curl up next to prominent DJs playing electronic music, attend hallucinogenic trance parties that have become associated with Goa, or sway to the beat of genres spanning the musical spectrum.

Bands and Live Music Venues

The live music scene in Goa is diverse, ranging from jazz and rock to fusion and reggae. Discover hidden jewels such as The Fisherman's Wharf, where local musicians and international stars set the scene for enthralling performances. Music unites disparate hearts in a symphony of sound in this instance, transcending language.

Midnight Madness and Beach Parties

Certain beaches are transformed into dance floors beneath the stars, with open-air parties that go all night. Curl your toes in the sand while swaying to a variety of tunes, or join the lively dance circles that erupt as the night progresses.

The Best Ways to Have an Unforgettable Night Out
Plan Ahead: Research events and parties happening during your stay. Many clubs host theme evenings or unique acts that may be of interest to you.

Dress the Part: Each venue has its vibe, so dress comfortably yet stylishly. Beachwear is appropriate for shacks, while clubs may demand somewhat more upmarket attire.

Safety First: Goa is known for its warm hospitality, but it's wise to keep an eye on your belongings and stay cautious, especially in crowded areas.

Exploring Goa's Nightlife Hotspots

Tito's Lane, Baga: A bustling strip lined with clubs and bars. Tito's is a well-known name in town, with multi-level dancing and live DJ performances.

Curlies Beach Shack, Anjuna: This seaside shack morphs into a colorful club complete with fire dancers and trippy rhythms.

LPK Waterfront, Nerul: This club, known for its unique atmosphere, overlooks the calm backwaters and provides an international music experience.

Britto's, Baga: A renowned beachfront place where you may dine by the water while listening to live bands and fusion music.

Practical Details
Opening Hours: Vary per location. Many beach shacks are open till late at night. Clubs often start about 10 p.m. and stay open into the early hours of the morning.

Average Cost: Entry fees to clubs vary from $10 to $30, depending on the event and location. Beach shacks are more affordable, with drinks and food costing between $15 and $25 per person.

Contacts: For the most up-to-date information on events, timetables, and entrance fees, visit the venues' respective websites or social media pages.

The night sky isn't the limit in Goa's nightlife; it's only the beginning. Immerse yourself in a nighttime trip that portrays the essence of Goa in all its colorful splendor, with the stars as your friends and the rhythms as your guide.

Clubs and Live Music Venues

When the moon rises and the sea breeze brings the promise of adventure, Goa's clubs and live music venues transform into the night's hub. The music is pulsing, the dance floors are shimmering, and the excitement fills the air. These venues are where the rhythm of the night takes center stage, whether you're a dance enthusiast, a music fan, or just looking for a taste of Goa's nighttime charm.

Clubbing: Dance to the Beat of Goa's Nightlife

Mambo's, Baga Beach

Mambo's, a real Tito's Lane icon, provides an unforgettable partying experience. Its dynamic ambiance, lively audience, and world-class DJs keep the dance floor alive into the early hours of the morning. Expect a night filled with EDM, trance, and mainstream songs.

HillTop, Vagator

HillTop, located on a hill overlooking Vagator, is a well-known psychedelic trance venue. Its Sunday parties have become a Goa staple, drawing partygoers from all over the globe. Allow the sounds and images to take you to another world under the stars.

Live Music Venues: Dance to the Night's Melody

Cohiba, Sinquerim

Cohiba is an excellent alternative for anyone looking for a mix of live music and a refined environment. The stage comes alive with great local and international musicians performing a range of genres such as jazz, blues, and reggae.

The Fisherman's Wharf, Salcette

This rustic restaurant and music venue, nestled on the banks of the River Sal, delivers heartfelt live performances. In this delightful atmosphere, you'll find yourself swaying to the beat of passionate ballads and vibrant folk music.

Making the Most of Your Night

Theme Nights: Many clubs have themed nights like retro, Bollywood, or trance. Check their calendars to make sure your visit coincides with a night that appeals to you.

Arrive Early: If a prominent DJ or band is playing, getting there early assures you obtain a nice location on the dance floor or a comfy seat with a decent view of the stage.

Dress the Part: Clubs usually have a dress code, and many live music venues have a relaxed yet stylish vibe. Appropriate attire enhances the whole experience.

Practical Details
Average Cost: Club admission fees vary from $10 and $30, and are occasionally inclusive of a set amount of drinks. There is usually no cover fee at live music venues, however, it is polite to purchase food or beverages.

Opening Hours: Clubs often open at about 10 p.m. and stay open till daybreak. Usually, live music venues start performing at about 8 p.m. and go late into the night.

Contacts: For the most up-to-date event information, timings, and entrance fees, visit the clubs' and venues' respective websites or social media pages.

Goa's nightlife becomes a dimension of pure bliss when the stars overhead sync with the sounds on the dance floor or the song on stage. These venues are more than simply places to have fun; they're portals to a dynamic and spectacular night in the heart of Goa's entertainment scene, whether you're dancing to the DJ's beat or swaying to the live band's melody.

Beach Parties and Other Nighttime Activities in Goa

As the sun sets, Goa's coastline turns into an enthralling tapestry of beach parties, open-air gatherings, and one-of-a-kind nighttime experiences. Aside from traditional clubs and live music venues, the beaches come alive with a distinct type of excitement, with the waves providing the beat and the stars setting the stage. Let us enter the enthralling world of beach parties and other unique nocturnal events that characterize Goa's bustling nightlife.

Beach Parties: Dancing Under the Stars

125

Anjuna Beach: Curlies and Shiva Valley

Anjuna's mystical aura extends to its beach parties, with Curlies and Shiva Valley being iconic names. These renowned shacks hold trance parties that draw visitors from all around the world. Dance barefoot on the beach beneath a starry sky to the sounds of the breaking waves.

Silent Noise at Palolem Beach

Palolem's Silent Noise parties are a one-of-a-kind experience. You may dance to your favorite DJ's songs using wireless headphones instead of traditional speakers, creating a dreamlike experience in which the music solely echoes inside your ears.

Midnight Madness: Raves and Flea Markets

Arpora Saturday Night Market

Arpora's Saturday Night Market evolves into a bustling carnival of shopping, live music, and exquisite street food once the sun goes down. Under a starlit sky, explore the unique booths, dance to live music, and savor the different food.

Raves in the Wilderness

Certain undiscovered places come alive with secret rave parties when bonfires light up the night and music creates an unfiltered connection between revelers and nature.

Practical Tips for Beach Parties and Others

Arrive Early for Sunset: Many beach parties begin in the evening, allowing you to enjoy Goa's breathtaking sunsets before the night's activities begin.

Dress comfortably: Beach parties have a laid-back attitude. Wear comfortable attire and footwear appropriate for sand dancing.

Cash and essentials: Bring cash for admission fees and shopping. Maintain the security of your stuff and avoid carrying too many valuables.

Practical Details

Average Cost: Entry fees for beach parties range from $5 to $20, depending on the area and event. The Saturday Night Market normally charges roughly $2 to enter.

Opening Hours: Beach parties often begin around sunset, while the Saturday Night Market begins in the late afternoon and runs until midnight.

Contacts: For the most up-to-date information on timings, venues, and entrance fees, visit the relevant event pages or local listings.

When the moon rises over Goa's beaches, the coastline comes alive with a symphony of celebrations that lasts all night. Whether you're dancing beneath the stars at a beach party, perusing the bright booths of the night market, or succumbing to the draw of a forest celebration, each encounter reveals a different aspect of Goa's after-dark fascination. Allow the waves to wash your worries away and the music to lead your feet as you enjoy the freedom of Goa's nightlife.

Hippie Scene

In the 1960s, the beaches of Goa welcomed a flood of free-spirited vacationers looking for more than simply a vacation; they were looking for a way of life. This period saw the beginning of the hippie movement in Goa, and the echoes of those revolutionary times may still be felt in the air today. Goa's hippie movement isn't just a sentimental past; it's a vibrant, breathing culture that shapes the lifestyle and atmosphere of this coastal paradise.

Recapturing the Hippie Spirit

Anjuna: The Hippie Heartbeat
Anjuna Beach, long a peaceful haven for seekers of enlightenment, has kept its bohemian air. Curlies Beach Shack has a colorful flea market on Wednesdays when craftsmen, visitors, and artists come to exchange handicrafts, jewelry, and ideas.

Arambol: A Bohemian Paradise

Arambol's allure stems from its peaceful beauty and creative culture. Drum circles, fire dancers, and acrobats often converge on the beach after dusk, providing a glimpse of the ancient and modern hippie cultures that coexist here.

Artistic Expression: Juggling, Drumming, and Other Activities

The hippie culture is all about expressing oneself. Juggling sessions, fire dances, and drum circles may be seen on several beaches, including Anjuna and Arambol. Participate or just watch as the beat of drums blends with the crash of waves.

Best Ways to Immerse in the Hippie Scene

Open Mindset: The hippie movement values variety and alternative lifestyles. Engage in interactions with other visitors and locals to get a better understanding of their viewpoints.

Respectful Exploration: While the hippie scene welcomes visitors, respect the community and its values.

Seek permission before participating in events such as drum circles.

Practical Details

Average Cost: Because the hippie lifestyle is generally about free-spirited gatherings, there are no admission fees. Consider supporting local craftsmen by buying their work.

Engagement Times: Hippie gatherings often take place after twilight or nights, with drum circles and fire dances beginning about sundown.

Embrace the Legacy

The Goa hippie scene is a fusion of nostalgia and development, where the past meets the present in a harmonic dance of cultures. You're following in the footsteps of folks who sought more than the ordinary, who embraced the rhythm of the cosmos and cherished life's basic pleasures as you explore the coasts of Anjuna and Arambol. The hippie culture in Goa allows you to recapture the spirit of a bygone period while creating fresh tales that will reverberate for years to come, whether you're producing jewelry at a flea market, participating in a drum circle, or just taking in the energy of the moment.

Chapter 8: Goa's Cultural Tapestry

Fairs and Festivals: Immerse in Goa's Celebrations

A rich and diversified assortment of fairs and festivals that reflect the essence of its people, traditions, and beliefs can be found in the core of Goa's unique cultural tapestry. From centuries-old religious processions to current music and art extravaganzas, Goa's calendar is jam-packed with events that not only celebrate the state's history but also weave a tapestry of social peace and shared delight.

Carnival: A Vibrant Extravaganza

Date: This event is usually held in February.
Location: All across Goa

The Goa Carnival, a lively carnival that merges Portuguese and Indian cultures, kicks off the year's festivities. Streets are decorated with bright floats, dancers, and music, culminating in the spectacular Red and Black dance at the conclusion. Wear masks and costumes and join in the fun as the stage explodes in a frenzy of dance, music, and joy.

Shigmo Festival: A Traditional Tapestry

Date: This event is usually held in March.
Location: Several towns and villages

The Shigmo Festival, which celebrates the entrance of spring, is a traditional Hindu festival that exhibits Goa's unique dance traditions, such as the Ghode Modni and Fugdi. Dancers dressed in bright costumes dance to the beat of traditional instruments, bringing mythology and culture to life.

Feast of St. Francis Xavier: A Spiritual Pilgrimage

Date: December 3rd
Location: Basilica of Bom Jesus, Old Goa

This solemn feast, held in honor of St. Francis Xavier, draws thousands of devotees and visitors to the Basilica of Bom Jesus in Old Goa. The saint's remains are on display for adoration, and a great parade through the streets, accompanied by songs and prayers, transports his statue.

Goa Arts and Literature Festival: A Creative Melange

Date: This event is usually held in December.
Location: Various venues

The Goa Arts & Literature Festival is a must-attend event for people interested in the arts. It brings together national and international artists, authors, and intellectuals to celebrate literature, music, theater, and visual arts. Participate in talks, workshops, and immerse yourself in a creative discourse that crosses borders.

Practical Tips for Festival Attendees

Research: Check out the festival dates and plan your trip appropriately. Some holidays are based on the lunar calendar, therefore double-check the dates.

Cultural Sensitivity: Respect the festival's customs and traditions. Maintain a reasonable distance and witness religious processions discreetly.

Local Cuisine: Festivals often include a variety of local foods. Savor real Goan tastes at traditional food booths.

Accessibility and Cost
Entry fees for festivals vary. The Goa Carnival and Shigmo Festival are normally free to attend, however, certain events may have small entrance fees.

The festival and event determine the opening hours. It's a good idea to double-check the schedule ahead of time.

Immersion in Goa's festivities is a trip through time, culture, and spirituality. Each festival creates a story that connects the past with the present, from the exuberant

136

rhythms of Carnival to the elaborate dance forms of Shigmo. As you participate in the cultural symphony that vibrates through the streets and hearts of Goa, embrace the vivid colors, beautiful songs, and community spirit that distinguish these festivals.

Music, Dance, and Theater: Cultural Performances

Goa's cultural tapestry is embellished with a vibrant assortment of music, dance, and theater performances that represent the spirit of its rich heritage, in addition to its magnificent beaches and historical buildings. Goa's stages come alive with a dazzling symphony of creative storylines, ranging from ancient art forms entrenched in tradition to modern expressions that mix cultures.

Folk Dances: The Rhythm of Tradition
Fugdi and Dhalo: Fugdi and Dhalo are traditional Goan folk dances performed by ladies that celebrate rustic charm. Dancers in vibrant costumes flow smoothly to the

beat of traditional music, expressing tales of everyday life, nature, and love.

Ghode Modni: During the Shigmo Festival, this horse dance depicts the bravery of Goan soldiers. Dancers in colorful costumes imitate horse motions while playing out war scenarios to the rhythm of traditional instruments.

Lamp Dance: An amazing art form, Lamp Dance features dancers balancing lighted lights on their heads while they move in unison. It is often done during religious festivals and special events.

Theater and Dramatics: Stories on Stage
Tiatr: Tiatr is Goa's unique type of theater, combining drama, music, and satire to highlight social and political concerns. Tiatr houses have witnessed generations of performers and spectators, and the performances are in Konkani.

Natak and Khell: Traditional dramas and comedic plays, known as Natak and Khell, have been part of the Goan culture for centuries. They investigate moral precepts and cultural processes, often combining wit and wisdom.

Contemporary Expressions: Cultural Fusion
Goa World Music Festival: Celebrating diversity and international collaborations, this festival brings together musicians from around the world to fuse their genres into a unique sonic experience.

Konkani Rock and Pop: The modern music industry in Goa is diversified, with performers fusing Konkani lyrics with rock, pop, and electronic sounds to produce a fusion that appeals to a younger audience.

Practical Tips for Enjoying Cultural Performances
Event Listings: Check local event listings or ask residents for information about upcoming cultural performances and shows.

Venue: Many performances take place in community centers, theaters, and parks. Before you travel, confirm the location and times.

Support Local Artists: Many of these performances are by local artists. Attend to show your support for their skills and to help preserve Goan culture.

Accessibility and Cost

The cost of tickets for cultural performances varies according to the event and venue. Folk dance performances in small towns are often free to attend, although theater performances and festivals may have admission fees.

Depending on the event, opening and closing hours vary. It is best to check the schedule and come early to get a decent seat.

You're invited to experience a cultural tapestry woven with tales, music, and movements handed down through generations when the curtains rise on Goa's stages. Each performance reveals a chapter of Goa's creative history, from the ancient rhythms of folk dances to the present beats of global music festivals. Allow yourself to be taken into a world where tradition dances hand in hand with innovation, leaving you enthralled by the harmonic symphony of culture as the lights darken and the music starts.

Highlighting Goa's Vibrant Festivals

Throughout the year, Goa's cultural canvas explodes into brilliant colors as its festivals cover the towns and villages with a tapestry of festivities, rites, and spiritual zeal. These celebrations capture the spirit of Goa's eclectic heritage, fusing religious devotion, communal cohesion, and raucous joy. Let us enter the mosaic of Goa's colorful festivals, each a distinct brushstroke that contributes to the masterpiece of its cultural tapestry.

Shigmotsav: Goa's Colorful Carnaval

Date: This event is usually held in March.

Location: All across Goa

Shigmotsav, Goa's equivalent of Holi, is a colorful frenzy of music and dance. The celebrations, which last a month, include traditional folk dances, street processions, and colorful floats. Villagers dressed in eye-catching costumes dance to the beat of drums to celebrate the triumph of virtue over evil.

Sao Joao Festival: Dive into Joy

Date: June 24th
Location: Throughout Goa, particularly in Siolim

Sao Joao, dedicated to St. John the Baptist, is a unique celebration that involves jumping into wells and water bodies. The custom is said to honor the saint's jump of delight in his mother's womb upon meeting the Virgin Mary. Revelers wear bright crowns, sing and dance, and take part in boisterous feasts.

Diwali: Lighting Up the Night

Date: 12th November

Location: Across Goa

Diwali, or the Festival of Lights, is very important to Goan Hindus. Oil lamps, candles, and colorful rangoli decorations decorate homes. Fireworks illuminate the night sky, as families gather to rejoice, share sweets, and pray.

Christmas: A Joyous Season

Date: December 25th

Location: Across Goa

Christmas is widely celebrated in Goa, because of its Portuguese heritage. Churches are lavishly decorated, and midnight Mass is a spectacular spectacle, followed by celebrations, eating, and gift-giving.

Practical Tips for Festivals

Cultural Sensitivity: While most festivals are accessible to the public, guests should respect the event's holiness and traditions. To truly immerse oneself, follow local traditions and practices.

Festival Dates: For correct festival dates, consult the lunar calendar, since certain events are based on lunar phases.

Local Cuisine: Festivals often include a variety of traditional meals. Enjoy the local food to get the full flavor of the festivities.

Accessibility and Cost

Festivals in Goa, particularly those hosted in public locations, are often free to attend.
The festival and event have different opening and ending timings. It's advisable to verify with locals for exact schedules for processions and celebrations.

Festivals in Goa are more than simply days on a calendar; they are chapters in the region's history that show the confluence of cultures, beliefs, and celebrations. You are not only a spectator but a participant in the energetic symphony of Goa's cultural heritage as you immerse yourself in the vivid processions, dance to the rhythms of folk music, and experience the communal spirit of festivals.

Chapter 9: Gastronomic Journey in Goa

Savoring Goa's Culinary Treasures

Exploring Goa's cuisine is like tracking the growth of a region's history and culture via its tastes. Goa's food is a complex tapestry woven with influences from indigenous populations, Portuguese conquerors, and a diverse mix of foreign tourists. Every dish, from hot curries to delightful desserts, is a chapter in this culinary voyage that encourages you to enjoy the state's heart and soul.

Rice and Fish: The Goan Staple

Fish Curry Rice: This renowned meal exemplifies Goa's seaside richness. A zesty coconut-based curry is served with rice and complemented with a variety of fish, all of which contribute to a flavorful symphony.

Xacuti: Elegance and Spice

This flavorful curry is made with roasted spices, coconut, and soft bits of meat (chicken, lamb, or hog). As a consequence, the taste profile is rich and dances on the tongue, reflecting the profundity of Goan cuisine.

Feni: The Spirit of Goa

Feni, a strong indigenous spirit derived from cashew apples, represents Goa's dynamic vitality. It may be consumed alone or in traditional cocktails such as the Feni Colada, a Goan spin on the original Pia Colada.

Bebinca: Layers of Sweet Delight

Bebinca, a tiered coconut milk pudding with ghee, sugar, and nutmeg, is a dish that screams luxury. Each layer is a sensory trip of texture and flavor—a suitable end to any Goan dinner.

Practical Culinary Exploration Tips

Local Eateries: For a true taste of Goan food, seek out local eateries and street sellers. These hidden treasures often deliver the most tasty and authentic food.

Levels of Spiciness: Goan food may be spicy. If you're sensitive to spice, remember to ask for a milder version.

Seafood Feast: If you're a seafood enthusiast, explore the many shacks along the coast for a true feast of fresh catches.

Culinary Adventures and Cost
Lunch at neighborhood eateries may cost between $5 and $15 per person on average. Fine dining restaurants may charge a premium.

Must-Try Activities: Take a cooking lesson to understand the secrets of Goan delicacies and bring a taste of Goa home with you.

Goa's food industry has something for everyone, from modest local eateries to sophisticated restaurants. You're not simply eating a meal when you appreciate the fusion of flavors and ingredients unique to this area; you're experiencing history, tradition, and innovation all on a single plate. So, go out on this culinary adventure with an open heart and an empty stomach, and let Goa's culinary riches bloom before you in a symphony of flavor and perfume.

Must-Try Goan Dishes

Goan cuisine is a captivating mix of local ingredients, Portuguese influences, and seaside bounty. As a consequence, a compelling assortment of foods tantalizes taste receptors while painting a picture of the region's rich cultural heritage. To fully experience the spirit of Goa, go on a gastronomic voyage via its must-try meals, each of which is a work of art in its own right.

Vindaloo: A Spicy Delight
This traditional Goan meal exemplifies the region's love affair with spices. Slow-cooked marinated meat (typically pork) with a spicy combination of red chilies, vinegar, and fragrant spices. The end product is a taste symphony that is sour, spicy, and irresistibly delectable.

Sorpotel: A Flavor Melange

Sorpotel, a meal made with pork and offal and cooked with a combination of spices and vinegar, is a real depiction of Goa's varied heritage. It's a popular celebratory meal that's substantial, savory, and a staple of Goan festivities.

Bhaji Pav: Street Food Heaven

Bhaji Pav, a Goan street food staple, is a delicious vegetable curry eaten with soft bread rolls called Pav. This meal represents the blend of flavors that distinguishes Goan cuisine.

Fried Fish: Pure Delight

Goa's coastline provides an abundance of seafood. The technique of perfectly frying fish is a culinary legacy here. Savor the freshness and crispiness of the catch in beach shacks or local eateries.

Practical Gastronomic Exploration Tips

Local Recommendations: Ask locals where they like to eat traditional Goan cuisine. They'll point you in the direction of hidden treasures and family-run businesses.

Spice Adventure: Embrace the spices, but if you're not used to them, ask for a lighter version of the meal.

Culinary Tours: Participating in a culinary tour is a great chance to try a variety of Goan cuisine while learning about their history and preparation.

Culinary Experiences and Cost
Average Cost: Prices for these must-try foods vary, but a dinner incorporating one of these meals will typically cost between $5 and $15 per person.

Cooking Class: Consider attending a cooking class to learn how to make these meals at home and to understand the methods used in Goan cooking.

Goa's culinary riches nurture the spirit as well as the body by telling the history, traditions, and tastes that distinguish the place. You're taking part in a centuries-old tradition of sharing food, culture, and love as you appreciate each dish. So, let your taste senses take you on an unforgettable trip, where each mouthful is an invitation to experience the essence of Goa's culinary tradition.

Beach Shacks to Fine Dining

The variety of gastronomic experiences available in Goa, from the rustic beauty of beach shacks to the grandeur of fine dining venues, is one of its many attractions. Goa's gourmet environment appeals to every taste bud, giving up superb meals against the background of magnificent coastlines and verdant environs.

Beach Shacks: Coastal Delights on the Waters

Location: Along the shore, on the beaches
Ambiance: Laid-back, casual, open-air
Must-Try: Fresh seafood, Goan curries, cocktails

Enjoy the relaxed atmosphere of Goa's beach shacks, where you may eat with your feet in the sand and the ocean wind on your skin. Curlies Beach Shack in Anjuna (www.curliesgoa.com, +91 98230 44777) offers a real coastal experience. While watching the surf, try their seafood platters and specialty cocktails.

Local Eateries: Flavors of Tradition and Community

Towns and villages serve as the setting.
Vibrant, local charm, buzzing atmosphere
Traditional Goan cuisine, thalis (platters), and street food are must-tries.

At local eateries, discover the essence of Goan cuisine. Vinayak Family Restaurant in Mapusa (www.vinayakfamilyrestaurant.com, +91 832 225 9360) serves classic Goan meals with bold spices. Don't miss their Goan fish curry and rice, or their exquisite thali, which combines a variety of genuine tastes on a single platter.

Gastronomy Takes Center Stage in Fine Dining

Setting: High-end resorts and freestanding restaurants

Ambiance: Elegant, sophisticated, intimate

Must-Try: Fusion dishes, gourmet seafood, international cuisine

For an elevated culinary experience, explore fine dining establishments. Gunpowder Restaurant & Bar (www.gunpowdergoa.com, +91 98232 67414) in Assagao provides a mix of tastes in a tranquil atmosphere. Indulge in their inventive meals that mix local ingredients with global influences, complemented by a well-picked wine selection.

Practical Culinary Exploration Tips

Reservations are often needed at fine eating establishments. Secure your place ahead of time to ensure a smooth experience.

Local Flavors: Savor the true flavor of Goa at local eateries. Explore lively marketplaces for Vada Pav and Bebinca, two popular street foods.

Beach shacks provide a laid-back atmosphere. Dress for the beach and sea comfortably.

Cost as well as Culinary Delights
Beach Shacks: A meal typically costs between $10 to $20 per person.

Local Eateries: Budget-friendly options range from $5 to $15 per person.

Fine Dining: Fine dining experiences start at $30 per person and might vary.

Goa's gastronomic range appeals to every desire, from the simple joys of seaside shacks to the refined enticement of gourmet dining. Every meal is an invitation to taste Goa's rich flavors while taking in its natural beauty, whether with the sea wind your hair or the middle of polished elegance.

Seafood Sensations

Goa's gastronomic identity is inextricably connected with the riches of the ocean since it is nestled along the Arabian Sea. The region's strong maritime history and coastal richness have resulted in a phenomenal seafood culture. Dining on seafood in Goa is a voyage of tastes that parallels the ebb and flow of the tides, from classic fish curries to inventive seafood dishes.

Fresh Catch: The Lifeblood of Goan Cuisine

Fish Curry Rice: A culinary anthem, this meal perfectly balances tastes. A sour coconut-based curry, frequently laced with kokum, tamarind, or raw mango, is served atop aromatic rice and the day's freshest catch.

Rava Fried Fish: The fish is covered in a semolina crust and fried to crispy golden perfection. The end effect is a lovely texture contrast that enables the natural tastes of the fish to show through.

Caldeirada: The Seafood Stew

Caldeirada, which has Portuguese origins, is a seafood blend cooked in a tomato and wine-based broth. This fragrant stew has a variety of seafood, including prawns, squid, and mussels, all peacefully blending in a sea of rich flavors.

Crab Xec Xec: A Goan Classic

The dish Crab Xec Xec illustrates the intricacy of Goan cuisine. The crab is cooked in a rich stew containing roasted spices, coconut, and tamarind, resulting in a sweet and savory meal with a touch of tanginess.

Practical Seafood Exploration Tips

Freshness is important: Choose eateries recognized for their fresh seafood. Look for the catch of the day and inquire about its provenance.

Seasonal Delights: Some seafood kinds are only available during certain seasons. Inquire about the optimal time to enjoy certain meals.

Local Specialties: Speak with locals to find hidden treasures that serve real seafood meals. Their suggestions often result in amazing feasts.

Culinary Experiences and Cost
Average Cost: Seafood dishes in local eateries usually range from $10 to $20 per person.

Specialty Restaurants: Prices vary depending on the kind of seafood and the atmosphere of the restaurant.

From humble fishing villages to upscale restaurants, seafood reigns supreme in Goa. You are enjoying more than just tastes when you delight in the abundance of the ocean—you are connecting with the maritime heritage that has created Goa's culinary character. So, start on this seafood adventure, and let each taste transport you along the waves of tradition, creativity, and the simple pleasure of appreciating the sea's treasures.

Where to Eat in Goa

Knowing where to discover the greatest culinary experiences in Goa is essential for generating lasting memories as you begin on your gastronomic trip around the state. Whether you're looking for local cuisine, international cuisine, or seaside treats, Goa's eclectic eating scene has something for everyone. Allow this guide to take you to some of the best restaurants in the area.

Local Eateries: Authentic Flavors and Vibrant Markets

Vinayak Family Restaurant, Mapusa: A local gem renowned for traditional Goan dishes and thalis. In the heart of Mapusa, taste the authentic flavor of Goan food. +91 832 225 9360, www.vinayakfamilyrestaurant.com.

Gunpowder Restaurant and Bar, Assagao: A blend of global influences with local ingredients, offering Mediterranean and Asian delights. At this colorful venue, you may immerse yourself in a world of tastes. Gunpowder Goa, +91 98232 67414.

Suzie, Panaji: An Asian gastronomic wonderland with everything from sushi to Thai curries. Suzie offers a complex combination of Asian spices. Suziegoa, www.suziegoa.com, +91 74474 44533.

Cantare Restaurant, Saligao: A taste of Europe in Goa, with hearty pasta and wood-fired pizzas, among other things. This beautiful restaurant offers a warm European atmosphere. Cantare, www.cantare.in, +91 98503 77772.

Beach Shacks: Relaxation by the Waters

Curlies Beach Shack, Anjuna: A renowned beachfront hangout serving fresh seafood and cocktails with a view of the ocean. Enjoy superb seaside dining at its best. Curlies Goa, +91 98230 44777.

Palolem's Baba's Wood Cafe: A rustic beach shack serving wonderful seafood that captures the authentic

160

character of Palolem. Enjoy the beach ambiance of Palolem while tasting seafood delicacies.

Fine Dining: Culinary Elegance and Sophistication

Gunpowder Restaurant and Bar, Assagao: A testament to culinary creativity, offering a fusion of global flavors in an elegant ambiance. Take pleasure in a refined eating experience. Gunpowder Goa, +91 98232 67414.

Black Sheep Bistro, Panaji: An exquisite fine dining establishment known for its artistic dishes and curated wine selection. Enhance your Panaji eating experience. +91 832 222 2901 (www.blacksheepbistro.in).

Verandah, Panaji: A blend of colonial charm and modern sophistication, offering a range of global cuisines. Dine in Panaji amongst luxury. Verandah, www.verandah.in, +91 83088 79161.

Practical Culinary Exploration Tips

Reservations: To guarantee a flawless experience, make reservations for fine restaurants and expensive places.

Diverse Experiences: For a well-rounded gastronomic trip, try a combination of local eateries, beach shacks, and fine dining.

Local Recommendations: Talk to locals about secret culinary jewels and real experiences that aren't often included in guidebooks.

Culinary Experiences and Cost
Average Cost: Low-cost alternatives vary from $5 to $20 per person, while upscale dining experiences may cost between $30 and $60 per person.
Diverse Atmosphere: Each restaurant has a distinct ambiance that adds to the eating experience.

Whether you want to enjoy local customs, cosmopolitan cuisines, or the allure of seaside eating, Goa's gastronomic map is your ticket to a memorable culinary adventure. Use this guide to help you navigate the dynamic eating scene and enjoy every dish in a setting that suits your likes and preferences.

Chapter 10: Wellness and Relaxation: Rejuvenation in Goa

Yoga and Inner Harmony: Exploring Goa's Wellness Centers

Goa emerges as a caring cocoon for people seeking inner peace and restoration among the lush landscapes and calming ocean breezes. The region's wellness facilities, which are strongly steeped in yoga, meditation, and holistic treatment techniques, provide a sanctuary where you may realign your mind, body, and spirit. Begin a transforming journey of self-discovery by immersing yourself in the traditional traditions compassionately provided by Goa's wellness establishments.

Yoga and Meditation for Serenity

Setting: tranquil settings with specific wellness facilities
Experience: Daily yoga classes, meditation sessions, spiritual workshops

Benefits: Stress relief, increased flexibility, mental clarity

Purple Valley Yoga Retreat, Assagao: This resort in Assagao is a refuge for yoga devotees. Daily classes, meditation sessions, and spiritual teachings foster an atmosphere of introspection and progress. Yogagoa, www.yogagoa.com, +91 98231 40204.

Ashiyana Yoga Retreat Village, Mandrem: This enchanting village-style retreat on Mandrem Beach offers a holistic approach to well-being. Accept regular yoga classes, meditation sessions, and workshops for all levels of practice. www.ashiyana.com or call +91 832 226 8200.

Ayurveda & Holistic Wellness

Setting: Ayurveda centers, serene retreats
Experience: Ayurvedic therapies, customized wellness consultations
Benefits: Holistic healing, detoxification, rejuvenation

Swaswara, Gokarna: While not in Goa, this adjacent healing sanctuary is worth mentioning. Swaswara, a short drive from Goa, provides tailored Ayurvedic treatments, yoga, meditation, and holistic wellness consultations. www.swaswara.com, +91 94489 75766.

The Mandala, Palolem: The Mandala offers a holistic approach to well-being. This serene retreat offers the perfect setting for your rejuvenation journey with yoga, meditation, and Ayurvedic therapies. http://www.themandalagoa.com/, +91 77986 85391.

Practical Wellness Exploration Tips

Book in Advance: Wellness facilities often have limited availability. Make a reservation for classes and sessions in advance.

Variety of Practices: Choose a center that offers a variety of yoga styles and meditation techniques to suit your preferences.

Local Cultural Sensitivity: When practicing yoga and meditation in public places, be mindful of local customs.

Transformation and Cost
Average Cost: Yoga and meditation classes are priced around $10 to $20 per session. Ayurvedic therapies may cost between $50 and $150 each session.

The wellness facilities in Goa provide a blank canvas for self-discovery and holistic development. Immerse yourself in the transforming techniques of yoga, meditation, and Ayurveda as you seek your inner sanctuary in the serene settings of Goa. Allow the region's peaceful spirit to take you to a deeper feeling of well-being, harmony, and renewal.

Spa Serenity: Embarking on a Journey of Rejuvenation

Goa's serene beaches not only soothe the soul but also provide a pathway to deep relaxation and renewal via its excellent spa experiences. World-class spas are housed in the region's luxury resorts and beachside hideaways, inviting you to rest, replenish your energy, and emerge invigorated. Prepare to be immersed in the world of spa peace and enjoy Goa's ultimate pampering experience.

A Relaxation Symphony

Setting: Luxury resorts, beachfront retreats
Experience: Spa treatments, holistic therapies, and relaxation routines
Benefits: Rejuvenation, relaxation, inner peace

The Leela Spa, Cavelossim: This spa sanctuary is nestled inside the sumptuous surroundings of The Leela Goa and brings you to a world of tranquility. Choose from a variety of excellent therapies, ranging from Ayurvedic treatments to aromatherapy massages, all suited to your specific requirements. www.theleela.com, +91 832 662 1234.

Sohum Spa, Candolim: A tranquil oasis within Novotel Goa Resort and Spa, Sohum Spa offers a blend of modern and traditional therapies. From body wraps to facials, leave it all in the hands of therapists who create customized experiences. www.novotelgoa.com, +91 832 249 4848.

The Mandala, Palolem: The Mandala welcomes you to go on a rejuvenation journey with its holistic technique for well-being. Discover distinctive therapies including Ayurvedic massages and holistic massages in the serene setting of Palolem Beach. www.themandalagoa.com, +91 77986 85391.

Making Your Spa Experience Unique

Select a spa that reflects your chosen degree of luxury, from holistic therapies to cosmetic treatments.

Appointment Scheduling: Reserve your chosen time in advance by booking spa treatments.

Personalization: Many spas provide individualized consultations to adapt treatments to your specific requirements.

The Cost of Rejuvenation

Average Cost: Depending on the style and length of the treatment, spa treatments may cost anywhere from $50 to $200 for each session.

Feel the weight of the world melt away as you surrender to the hands of professional therapists, and allow the serene environment of Goa's spas to wrap you in a cocoon of tranquility. Allow yourself the luxury of rejuvenation as you go on a trip that not only revitalizes your body but also feeds your spirit, leaving you with a refreshed feeling of well-being and equilibrium.

Chapter 11: Shopping and Souvenirs

Introduction to the Shopping Scene in Goa

Goa's thriving and diversified commercial environment reflects the state's rich cultural tapestry and various influences. From lively markets to boutique shops, the area has a wide range of shopping options to suit every taste and inclination. Whether you're looking for traditional handicrafts, modern fashion, or one-of-a-kind souvenirs, Goa's shopping districts guarantee an amazing shopping experience. Prepare to discover the many treasures that await you in this shopper's paradise.

Market Marvels: Uncovering Goa's Shopping Treasures

Anjuna Flea Market: This legendary market, held every Wednesday, is a treasure trove of handicrafts, clothing, jewelry, and international products. Dive into a vibrant

171

labyrinth of booths filled with craftsmen, visitors, and vendors. Remember to bargain for the best bargains and enjoy the lively environment.

Mapusa Market: A daily market in Mapusa, this is a center of local life where you can buy fresh vegetables, spices, textiles, and household products. As you tour the crowded booths, immerse yourself in the true Goan market experience and mingle with locals.

Calangute Market Square: This lively market sells everything from clothing and accessories to souvenirs. It's a terrific spot to shop for presents and souvenirs, as well as to soak in the vibrant ambiance of a Goan market.

Unique Finds at Boutiques and Art Galleries

Tuk Tuk Designs, Assagao: This boutique offers a diverse selection of clothing, accessories, and home décor, all with a boho flare. Tuktuk Designs, www.tuktukdesigns.in, +91 95525 27395.

Literati Bookshop & Cafe, Calangute: This beautiful bookshop provides a handpicked assortment of literature, art, and poetry for book lovers. Bring home a bit of Goa's literary culture. +91 98230 08788, www.literatibookshop.com.

Hunt & Gather, Sangolda: This concept shop offers a carefully chosen variety of home décor, clothing, and accessories, with an emphasis on local artists and modern designs. +91 93728 57124, www.huntandgathergoa.com.

Practical Shopping Exploration Tips

Bargaining Skills: Haggling is a common practice in markets, so embrace your negotiating skills for the best deals.

Cash and Cards: Markets often prefer cash, so bring enough local currency for your shopping trip.

Local Artisans: Support local artisans by purchasing handicrafts and products that reflect Goan traditions.

Cost and Shopping Experience
Average Cost: Market prices can vary significantly based on your bargaining skills. There may be set pricing in boutiques and galleries.

Prepare to be blown away by Goa's retail scene's diversity and attractiveness. Each shopping area, from bustling flea markets to boutique gems, gives a unique peek into the region's cultural richness. Goa's shopping experiences offer to enhance your vacation with treasured treasures and memories, whether you're seeking fashion statements, creative works, or genuine souvenirs.

Market Marvels: Navigating the Bustling Bazaars

Explore Goa's busy bazaars and immerse yourself in the vivid center of its cultural and commercial tapestry.

These dynamic markets are more than simply shopping destinations; they are energetic centers where you can connect with the local way of life, discover genuine crafts, and bring home one-of-a-kind souvenirs that capture the soul of your Goa journey. Each market provides a riveting tour into the region's active and diversified shopping environment, from lovely handicrafts to pungent spices.

Anjuna Flea Market: A Bohemian Paradise

Location: Anjuna
Operating Day: Every Wednesday
Highlights: Handicrafts, clothing, jewelry, live music
Atmosphere: Bohemian, lively, eclectic

Anjuna's famed flea market is a cultural phenomenon that has drawn both tourists and dealers for decades. This colorful and creative kaleidoscope comprises a variety of vendors selling anything from colorful fabrics and bohemian apparel to homemade jewelry and artistic artwork. Immerse yourself in the busy atmosphere, interact with merchants, and don't forget to enjoy the live music that adds to the market's bohemian character.

Mapusa Market: Embracing Local Life

Location: Mapusa
Operating Days: Daily Highlights: Fresh produce, spices, textiles, clothing
Atmosphere: Authentic, local, vibrant

The bustling Mapusa Market is a must-see Goan experience that immerses you in the pulse of everyday life. Locals shop here for fresh fruit, fragrant spices, and traditional fabrics. Stroll through the labyrinth of booths, mingle with sellers, and soak up the real atmosphere as you learn about the tastes and colors that distinguish Goan food and culture.

Calangute Market Square: A Shopper's Paradise

Location: Calangute

Operating Days: Daily Highlights: Clothing, accessories, souvenirs

Atmosphere: Active, Busy, and Tourist-Friendly

Calangute Market Square has a broad choice of shopping pleasures that appeal to both visitors and locals. This market is a treasure trove for visitors looking for mementos to memorialize their Goa trip, with everything from fashionable fashion and accessories to a profusion of souvenirs. Enjoy the bustling environment, peruse the many booths, and bring home a bit of the region's colorful spirit.

Practical Bazaar Exploration Tips

Haggling: Bargaining is customary in these markets, so hone your negotiation skills for the best deals.

Local Tastes: Sample local snacks and street cuisine for a true sense of Goan tastes while you shop.

Cultural Etiquette: Respect local customs and practices while interacting with vendors and fellow shoppers.

Navigating Goa's crowded bazaars is an engrossing adventure that provides insight into the region's cultural vitality and local lives. Whether you're looking for one-of-a-kind handicrafts, enjoying scented spices, or just immersing yourself in the local culture, each market offers a chance to connect with Goa's heritage and depart with treasured keepsakes of your adventure.

Souvenirs to Bring Home

No trip is complete until you have a collection of souvenirs that capture the memories and soul of your excursion. When it comes to significant souvenirs, Goa's colorful culture, rich history, and creative traditions provide a wealth of alternatives. Whether you're looking for traditional crafts, creative works, or daily memories, here's a handpicked list of Goa souvenirs that will last a lifetime.

Culinary Souvenirs: Feni and Other Delights

Feni: A famous local liquor created from cashew apples or coconut sap, Feni is Goa's indigenous spirit. Bring a bottle of Feni home to enjoy the tastes of Goa's distinct culture.

Spices: Bring a sense of Goa to your culinary adventures by acquiring locally produced spices such as turmeric, cardamom, and cinnamon.

Cashew Nuts: Cashew nuts are famous in Goa. Choose from salted and roasted, spicy, and chocolate-covered varieties.

Cultural Keepsakes: Traditional Crafts
Azulejos: These intricately painted Portuguese tiles are a testament to Goa's colonial past. Decorate your house with these magnificent pieces of art.

Folk Art: Take home colorful, hand-painted masks, figures, and traditional Goan art that exemplifies the region's diverse cultural heritage.

Handicrafts: Visit the markets to find a variety of fabrics, jewelry, and accessories made by local craftsmen.

Artistic Creations: Creative Remembrances
Art Galleries: Purchase paintings, sculptures, and other artworks that depict the beauty of Goa's scenery and culture to support local artists.

Pottery & Ceramics: Discover one-of-a-kind pottery and ceramic goods that represent the workmanship and creativity of Goan artists.

Fashion and Accessories: Stylish Memories

Clothing: From boho dresses to beachwear, take home fashionable items that exemplify Goa's free-spirited culture.

Jewelry: Explore intricate silver jewelry inspired by Goan traditions, with styles ranging from modern to traditional.

Practical Souvenir Shopping Tips

Authenticity: Look for authorized stores and galleries that feature real local art and crafts.

Cultural Sensitivity: When acquiring religious items or symbols, keep their meaning and cultural sensitivity in mind.

Packaging: Make sure delicate products are securely wrapped so they can make the trip back home.

Cost and Treasured Memories

Cost: Prices vary depending on the sort of memento and its authenticity. Traditional crafts and artworks might cost anything from $10 to $100 or more.

Remember that each item you choose conveys a bit of the region's personality while you shop the markets, galleries, and boutiques of Goa. These souvenirs not only depict Goa's creative heritage and colorful culture, but they also serve as physical recollections of the

Chapter 12: 7-Day Goa Adventure Itinerary

Day 1: Arrival and Introduction to Goa

Morning: Your adventure starts as you land at Dabolim Airport in Goa. The warm tropical breeze greets you as you enter this paradise. After passing through immigration and baggage claim, you're ready to enter the vivid tapestry that is Goa. Pre-arranged airport transfers supplied by your selected accommodation are convenient and comfortable.

Afternoon: Take a leisurely walk along the surrounding beach or explore the local neighborhood while you relax in your hotel. Get to know your surroundings by inhaling the salty air and taking in the relaxed environment. Enjoy a magnificent Goan lunch, relishing the tastes of traditional delicacies that will set the tone for your gastronomic adventure.

Evening: Visit one of Goa's famous beaches, such as Calangute or Baga, to watch the sunset over the Arabian Sea. Feel the sand under your feet and take in the coastal beauty as the sun paints the sky in orange and pink colors. As the evening progresses, enjoy the bustling atmosphere of beachside shacks and eateries while indulging in delicious seafood and socializing with other tourists.

Night: Unwind from your day of travel with a leisurely walk down the beach, serenaded by the rhythmic murmur of the waves. This is also an excellent time to get acquainted with your itinerary for the days ahead. Retire to your accommodation and let the calming ambiance of Goa lull you into a well-deserved nap.

Recommended Places to Stay:
Budget: Zostel Goa, Anjuna Beach Website: www.zostel.com
Phone: +91 22 4896 0969

Mid-Range: Santana Beach Resort, Candolim

Website: www.santana-goa.com

Phone: +91 832 248 8500

Luxury: Alila Diwa Goa, Majorda

Website: www.alilahotels.com/diwagoa Phone: +91 832
274 6800

Practical Tips:

Confirm airport transfer details when making your
reservation to ensure a seamless arrival experience.

Take it easy the first day to adjust to the tropical climate
and time zone change.

Welcome to Goa, where your adventure will unfold in a
symphonic symphony of beaches, culture, and
experiences that will leave an unforgettable impact on
your soul. Allow the first day's charm, along with the
ease of airport transfers, to set the tone for the
experiences that await.

Day 2: Beachfront Bliss and Cultural Immersion

Morning: Awaken to the sound of breaking waves and the promise of another wonderful day in Goa. Begin your day with a relaxing stroll down the beach's golden sands, enjoying the soothing caress of the sea breeze. A taste of Goa's time-honored maritime culture may be seen when local fishermen head out to sea in traditional boats.

Breakfast: Enjoy a delicious seaside breakfast at your accommodation or a local café. As you fuel yourself for the day's travels, enjoy tropical fruits, freshly baked pastries, and aromatic coffee.

Mid-Morning: Venture to the vibrant Anjuna Flea Market, where a world of creativity and culture awaits. Explore the labyrinth of booths selling one-of-a-kind handicrafts, apparel, jewelry, and other items. Engage with craftsmen, learn about their skills, and find gifts that speak to your soul.

Lunch: Have a leisurely lunch by the sea at a local beach shack. Enjoy a feast of Goan delights, including seafood curries and exquisite vegetarian meals. Allow the tastes of Goa to penetrate your senses while dining among the coastal beauty.

Afternoon: Explore the center of Old Goa, a UNESCO World Heritage Site that tells the narrative of the region's rich history. Visit the Basilica of Bom Jesus, a baroque masterpiece that holds St. Francis Xavier's mortal remains. Explore Sé Cathedral and marvel at its magnificent architecture, which bears tribute to Goa's colonial heritage.

Evening: As the sun starts to fall below the horizon, go to a peaceful riverside location to see a breathtaking sunset. As the sky morphs into a canvas of vibrant colors, the Mandovi River provides a magnificent background. This calm encounter embodies the spirit of Goa's charm.

Dinner: Visit a beachside restaurant or a local eatery to sample more of Goa's gastronomic marvels. Allow your taste senses to go on an extraordinary voyage, from traditional Goan vindaloo to worldwide culinary pleasures.

Night: Return to your accommodation, taking with you the memories of a day steeped in beachfront bliss and cultural immersion. Consider the experiences that have already enhanced your trip, recognizing that there is much more to learn in the days ahead.

Practical Tips
Wear comfortable shoes for visiting the flea market and historical sites.

To keep energetic under the Goan sun, stay hydrated throughout the day.

Day 2 of your Goa adventure combines the element of leisure with cultural exploration. This day provides a variety of activities that highlight the many sides of this charming paradise, from the colorful market to the historical sites.

Day 3: Unveiling Goa's Nature and Hidden Gems

Morning: As you begin a day of exploring, take in the beauty of Goa's natural landscapes. Start your day with a substantial breakfast at your accommodation, refueling for the adventure ahead.

Time for an adventure: Visit Dudhsagar Waterfalls, a hidden jewel situated among beautiful forests. The road to the falls winds through mountainous terrain, which is generally best explored on an exciting jeep safari. The flowing waters of Dudhsagar, which translates to "Sea of Milk," provide a captivating view. Spend some time admiring the falls' grandeur and, if you're feeling adventurous, take a cool plunge in the natural pool.

Lunch: Have a picnic-style lunch in the middle of nature, either at the falls or at a scenic site along the route. As you appreciate your lunch, take in the tranquility and calm of the surroundings.

Afternoon: Visit Tambdi Surla Temple, a lesser-known beauty. This 13th-century wonder, dedicated to Lord Shiva, has superb Kadamba architecture that exemplifies Goa's historical importance. The secluded setting of the temple in the verdant Western Ghats adds to its charm.

Tea Break: Relax at a local tea shop while drinking aromatic chai and admiring the spectacular views of the surrounding hills.

Evening at Butterfly Beach: As the sun sets, make your way to the gorgeous Butterfly Beach, which is just a short boat ride away. This quiet beach is ideal for visitors looking for natural beauty. Admire the rainbow of hues as the sun sets beyond the horizon, producing a golden light on the beaches.

Dinner: Return to your accommodation, clean up, and go out for dinner at a quaint restaurant serving genuine Goan food.

Night: As you listen to the noises of the night, reflect on your day. The melody of the forest and the waves lapping at the coast soothe you to sleep.

Practical Tips
Wear comfortable attire and sturdy footwear appropriate for the jeep safari and temple exploration.

For the day's travels, bring sunscreen, bug repellant, and a reusable water bottle.

Day 3 reveals Goa's natural beauty's hidden secrets. This day enables you to connect with the region's pristine landscapes and explore the enchantment that lies beyond the well-trodden trails, from waterfalls to secluded temples and calm beaches.

Day 4: Adventure and Thrills

Morning: Get your adrenaline racing as you begin an exciting day of excursions. Begin your day with a healthy meal that will fuel you for the day ahead.

Water Sports Extravaganza: Visit Calangute Beach, one of Goa's premier water sports destinations. Enjoy a variety of exhilarating water activities, including parasailing and jet skiing, as well as banana boat rides and kayaking. The Arabian Sea's stunning blue waters set the tone for your aquatic adventures.

Lunch: Take a break from water sports and enjoy a beachside lunch at a shack with spectacular ocean views. Savor the day's fresh fish, accented with local tastes that tempt your taste buds.

Afternoon Adventure: Set off on a trekking trip to the exciting Devil's Canyon, which is situated near Palolem Beach. This hike provides spectacular views of lush forests, secret waterfalls, and rock formations. It's an opportunity to reconnect with nature and discover Goa's wild side.

Tea Break: Take a refreshing tea break in the middle of nature's tranquility. Breathe in the fresh air and let the serenity of your surroundings watch over you.

Sunset Cruise: As the day turns to twilight, take a quiet sunset cruise around Goa's calm backwaters. Sip cool beverages while capturing the stunning colors of the setting sun painting the sky.

Dinner by the Sea: Return to the seaside for dinner and choose a beachfront restaurant. Allow the sound of the waves and the aroma of the sea to complement your eating experience.

Nightlife Adventure: Embrace Goa's vibrant nightlife by exploring its dance floors and entertainment venues. Whether it's a beach party, a live music show, or an energetic club, Goa's nightlife culture provides something for everyone.

Practical Tips

For water activities and trekking, dress comfortably and use proper footwear.

Pack a change of clothing, sunscreen, and swimsuits for the day's activities.

A rush of adventure and excitement awaits you on Day 4. This day is meant to satiate your need for excitement, from flying over the waves to trekking through breathtaking landscapes. Embrace Goa's dynamic character as you navigate from water activities to trekking trails and end the evening with lively nightlife.

Day 5: Wellness and Relaxation

Morning Yoga: Start your day off right with a rejuvenating yoga session on the beach or in a peaceful health center. The lovely murmur of waves and the delicate touch of the early light provide the ideal ambiance for an energizing practice that feeds both the body and the soul.

Breakfast: Start your day with a hearty breakfast that will help you on your wellness path. To begin your day on a healthy note, choose fresh fruits, wholesome grains, and herbal teas.

Wellness Retreat: Immerse yourself in the relaxing realm of wellness by treating yourself to a spa treatment or a refreshing massage. Goa has a plethora of wellness centers where you may rest your mind and body with Ayurvedic therapies, traditional massages, and holistic treatments.

Lunch: Select a nutritious meal that supports your wellness objectives. Many Goa restaurants include organic, vegetarian, and vegan options that are as tasty as they are wholesome.

Afternoon nap: Follow the local custom of taking an afternoon nap or taking a leisurely walk along the beach. Allow yourself to relax and refresh.

Sunset Meditation: As the sun sets, locate a peaceful area by the beach or in nature for a tranquil sunset meditation. Connect with the natural rhythms of your surroundings and let go of any residual tension.

Dinner: Choose a light and balanced meal to round off your wellness-focused day. Investigate restaurants that provide wholesome salads, grilled seafood, and plant-based cuisine.

Candlelit Reflection: Create a soothing ambiance in your accommodation by lighting candles and enjoying a moment of quiet reflection. Use this time to write, read, or just enjoy the peace.

Practical Tips
Wear comfortable clothing suitable for yoga and relaxation activities.

Drink herbal teas and lots of water throughout the day to stay hydrated.

Day 5 is all about your health and relaxation. This day provides a holistic approach to recuperation, including yoga, spa treatments, meditation, and nutritional meals. Take advantage of the chance to pamper yourself and discover peace amid Goa's natural beauty.

Day 6: Cultural Immerse and Festive Celebrations

Morning Exploration: Start the day by strolling around the lovely streets of Fontainhas, Goa's Latin Quarter. Explore the small alleys dotted with colorful Portuguese-style residences, each one offering a tale about the region's rich history.

Breakfast: Treat yourself to a breakfast that combines local delicacies with international influences. Prepare your body for a day of cultural immersion and celebrations.

Local Workshops: Participate in workshops that offer insights into Goa's cultural heritage. From traditional Goan cooking classes to art workshops, these activities enable you to immerse yourself in the local culture.

Lunch at a Local Eatery: Head to a local eatery known for serving authentic Goan delicacies. Indulge in delicacies that capture the essence of Goan tastes and are created using time-honored recipes.

Explore Local Markets: Discover the vibrant local markets that come to life with a plethora of colors, scents, and sounds. Anjuna Flea Market and Mapusa Market are two fantastic options to explore and shop for souvenirs.

Evening Festivities: Immerse yourself in the enchantment of Goa's festivals and celebrations. Depending on the time of year, you may be able to participate in lively festivals such as Carnival, Shigmo, or Sao Joao. Colorful processions, traditional dances, and exuberant revelry are on display.

Dinner at a Festive Venue: Enjoy dinner at a venue that captures the festive spirit of Goa. During festivals, many restaurants and beachside shacks conduct special events, allowing you to eat in the heart of the celebrations.

Night Celebration: If there isn't an active festival, create your joyous ambiance. Find a boisterous beach party or a live music venue to dance the night away, experiencing Goa's dynamic nightlife.

Practical Tips
Check the local festival calendar to see if any celebrations are scheduled to coincide with your visit.

Actively participate in workshops and interact with people to immerse yourself in the local culture.

On Day 6, you'll be immersed in Goa's culture and seasonal celebrations. This day takes a deep dive into the traditions that make Goa special, from seeing heritage districts to participating in workshops and enjoying the delight of local festivals. Whether you attend a formal festival or create your own festive experience, the vivid energy of Goa will capture you.

Day 7: Farewell and Reflection

Morning: As your last day in Goa begins, take a minute to appreciate the natural beauty of the area. Take your time with breakfast, relishing the taste one final time.

Beachfront Tranquility: Spend your morning contemplating the beach in tranquility. Listen to the waves, feel the sand under your feet, and soak in the serene ambiance.

Reflect and Recharge: Take time to reflect on the incredible journey you've experienced over the past week. Allow yourself to revisit the moments that have made an effect on your heart, whether via writing, meditation or just sitting in quiet.

Lunch: For your last meal, choose a beachside café or a local diner. Allow the tastes of Goa to accompany your thoughts, resulting in a bittersweet symphony of taste and memory.

Last-minute Souvenirs: If you want to bring back any last souvenirs or presents, go around the local markets or boutiques for that specific memento.

Afternoon Leisure: Spend your last afternoon in Goa as you please. Make the most of your remaining hours by reading a book beneath a palm tree or indulging in a relaxing spa treatment.

Sunset Goodbye: As the sun starts to dip over the horizon, locate a quiet area to say farewell to Goa's spectacular sunsets. Keep the beauty of the moment and the memories you've made in mind.

Farewell Dinner: Choose a restaurant that holds a special place in your heart for your farewell dinner. Raise a glass to your remarkable adventures and fantastic journey.

Night Reflection: As you pack your belongings, take a minute to gaze up at the stars and wonder at the majesty of the cosmos. Reflect on the experiences, lessons, and relationships you've made while in Goa.

Practical Tips
Photograph your best moments so you may relive them later.

Plan ahead of time your transportation to the airport or your next location.

Your incredible Goa vacation comes to a close on Day 7. It's a day for introspection, appreciation, and thanks for the life events that have affected your soul. As you wave goodbye to this tropical paradise, bring Goa's soul with you, knowing that its beauty and charm will live on in your heart forever.

Chapter 13: Practical Information

Local Customs and Etiquette

When visiting the wonderful paradise of Goa, it is essential to get acquainted with the local traditions and etiquette to have a respectful and joyful experience. Here are some tips to help you guide your encounters with the friendly locals:

Greeting: A warm grin and courteous "Namaste" (pronounced nuh-mus-tay) with folded hands are customary. In more metropolitan locations, handshakes are also prevalent.

Dress Modestly: While Goa is known for its relaxed atmosphere, especially on the beaches, it's advisable to dress modestly when visiting religious sites or local neighborhoods. When entering temples or churches, cover your shoulders and knees.

Footwear: It is usual to take your shoes off before entering houses, temples, and certain stores. Look for signs or watch locals to determine when to remove your shoes.

Respect Religious Sites: Be polite while visiting temples or churches. Avoid touching religious symbols or accessing holy sites without authorization.

Photography: Always ask for permission before taking photographs of people, especially in rural or less touristy areas. If you don't ask beforehand, some locals may find it invasive.

Public Display of Affection: While Goa is relatively liberal, it's advisable to refrain from excessive public displays of affection, as a sign of respect for local sensitivities.

Bargaining: Bargaining is a regular behavior in markets, but it should be done courteously and respectfully. Keep in mind that a reasonable price helps both you and the vendor.

Tipping is customary, particularly at restaurants and for services like taxi trips or guided tours. While there is no set amount, it is typical to round up the bill or leave a 10% tip.

Greetings and gestures: It is customary in more rural places to welcome elders or those in positions of authority first. The "Indian head shake" - a delicate back-and-forth movement of the head - may seem perplexing at first, but it typically indicates agreement or comprehension.

Language: While many Goans speak English, a few native Konkani or Marathi words might help you make contacts and demonstrate respect for the local culture.

By following these local traditions and etiquettes, you will not only be able to explore Goa more easily, but you will also have the chance to interact with the locals on a deeper level. The soul of Goa is found not just in its landscapes, but also in its people and their manner of life.

Language, Handy Phrases and Communication Tips

A few words in the local languages may tremendously enrich your interactions with the locals and give a personal touch to your Goa vacation. While English is commonly spoken, attempting to communicate in the local tongue may go a long way. Here are some useful terms and communication strategies to help you get around:

Languages spoken: Konkani, Marathi, and English are the predominant languages spoken in Goa. English is commonly spoken, particularly in tourist regions, so you should have no problem interacting.

Greetings

- "Namaste" (nuh-mus-tay) - A respectful greeting with folded hands.
- "Kaise ho?" (kay-se ho?) - How are you?

Basic Phrases

- "Aap kaise hain?" (ahp kay-seh hain?) - How are you?
- "Dhanyavaad" (dhun-yuh-vahd) - Thank you.
- "Kripya" (kree-pyah) - Please.
- "Haan" (hahn) - Yes.
- "Nahin" (nah-heen) - No.
- "Kitna hai?" (kit-nah hai?) - How much is it?
- "Kahaan hai?" (kah-han hai?) - Where is it?

Numbers

- "Ek" (ek) - One
- "Do" (doh) - Two
- "Teen" (teen) - Three
- "Chaar" (char) - Four
- "Paanch" (pahnch) - Five
- "Chhah" (chhah) - Six
- "Saat" (saat) - Seven

- "Aath" (aath) - Eight
- "Nau" (nau) - Nine
- "Das" (dus) - Ten

Directions

- "Right" (right) - Right
- "Left" (left) - Left
- "Aage" (aa-geh) - Ahead
- "Peeche" (pee-chay) - Behind
- Food and Drinks:
- "Khana" (khah-na) - Food
- "Paani" (pa-nee) - Water
- "Chai" (chai) - Tea
- "Khaana khane ka sthal kahaan hai?" (khah-na kha-nay kah sthal kah-han hai?) - Where is the restaurant?

Tips for Effective Communication

Warm smiles are a global language that may cross any divide.

Point and Show: When words fail, gestures might be quite handy. Pointing and demonstrating your objective often works wonders.

Slow Down: Speak clearly and slowly, particularly if you're utilizing regional jargon.

Respectful Tone: When addressing elders or people in positions of power, use a courteous and respectful tone.

Learn Numbers: Knowing numbers might come in handy when negotiating rates, ordering meals, or requesting amounts.

Local Insights

If you want to engage with the locals, start up a discussion at markets, cafés, and smaller eateries. Locals are frequently eager to share their experiences and suggestions.

Learning a few words might lead to unexpected discussions and experiences. If you're visiting a rural town, for example, greeting the locals in their language may create a warm and friendly environment.

Remember that the soul of travel is in the relationships you make and the moments you enjoy with the people you meet. So, don't be afraid to immerse yourself in the local language and participate in the unique tapestry of cultures that Goa has to offer. Your efforts will undoubtedly be recognized and rewarded with smiles and cross-cultural dialogues.

Safety and Health Guidelines

Your safety is of the highest importance when you begin your Goa vacation. While Goa is usually regarded as secure for visitors, care must be taken to guarantee a safe and happy trip. Here are some safety and health considerations to remember throughout your stay:

Health Precautions

Hydration: The tropical environment of Goa may be draining, particularly during the hotter months. To keep hydrated, carry a reusable water bottle and consume lots of fluids.

Sun Protection: Because the sun may be harsh, use sunscreen liberally, wear a hat, and wear sunglasses to protect your eyes. Reapply sunscreen as needed throughout the day, particularly if you're going to the beach.

Mosquito Protection: While malaria is not a major worry in Goa, it is recommended to wear mosquito repellent, particularly at night, to avoid bites.

Food Safety: While enjoying Goa's gastronomic wonders, choose freshly prepared and well-cooked meals. Consume food from street stalls that may not meet hygienic regulations.

Travel Precautions

Document Safety: Make photocopies of important travel documents like your passport, visa, and driver's license. Keep them apart from the originals.

Local Laws and Regulations: Become acquainted with local laws and traditions to prevent unintended etiquette or legal offenses.

Emergency Contacts: Save local emergency phone numbers on your phone, such as the closest hospital, police station, and embassy or consulate of your country.

Water Safety

Swimming: While Goa's beaches are beautiful, swimming should be done with care. Always obey lifeguards' directions and keep an eye out for strong currents.

Water: Avoid waterborne infections by drinking only bottled or filtered water. Before drinking bottled water, make sure the seals are still intact.

Local Interaction

Respectful Behavior: Interact with locals respectfully, keeping in mind cultural differences and local customs.

Solo Travel: While Goa is relatively safe for solo travelers, avoid isolated areas after dark. Stay in densely populated, well-lit locations.

Medical Care

Medical Services: Although Goa has medical facilities and hospitals, it is recommended that you carry travel insurance that covers medical emergencies.

Medications: If you have specific medical needs, carry the necessary medications and a copy of your prescriptions.

Emergency Situations

Natural Disasters: During the monsoon season, Goa is prone to excessive rains. Follow weather predictions and authorities' guidance in case of severe weather.

Emergency Evacuation: In the event of an emergency evacuation, abide by the directions of local authorities and your lodging.

Practical Tips
Keep an eye on your surroundings and follow your instincts.

When renting a car, make sure it's in excellent shape and that you observe all road safety precautions.

By following these safety and health rules, you'll be well-prepared to enjoy your Goa vacation while maintaining your safety. Remember that the secret to a successful and safe travel experience is a balance of enthusiasm and caution.

Parking and Transportation Tips

Practical transportation and parking information make it easier to navigate Goa's various landscapes and vibrant towns. Whether you're traveling along the coastline or seeing interior treasures, the following advice will help you better grasp your choices for transportation and park convenience:

Strategies for Parking

Beach Parking: Many prominent beaches have dedicated parking areas with attendants to guide you. Expect to pay a little parking fee, which ranges between $1 and $2 depending on the beach and car type.

Market Areas: Parking may be difficult to find in crowded marketplaces. Plan to park a little farther away from crowded areas and walk to your destination.

Parking Attendants: Park attendants may approach you and offer to babysit your car for a modest fee. While not required, using their services may help to assist local people.

Tips for Driving

Traffic Regulations: Goa follows regular Indian traffic regulations. Always drive on the left side of the road and make sure everyone is wearing a seatbelt.

Road Conditions: Road conditions might vary, with potholes or uneven surfaces in certain regions. Be cautious, particularly during the monsoon season when roads might become slick.

Driving at Night: Be careful of limited visibility and the presence of pedestrians and bicycles while driving at night.

Insights into Public Transportation

Buses: Buses are an inexpensive and ecologically beneficial means of transportation. They may not be the fastest choice, but they provide a genuine local experience.

Auto-rickshaws: Auto-rickshaws are popular for short-distance travel. Pre-arrange fares or request that they utilize the meter.

Time Management

Traffic Peaks: Traffic congestion can intensify during peak tourist seasons, weekends, and public holidays. Make travel plans accordingly.

Monsoon Consideration: From June to September, the monsoon season can impact road conditions due to heavy rainfall. Allow for additional travel time and be cautious on wet roads.

By integrating these tips into your vacation arrangements, you'll be well-prepared to enjoy Goa's natural beauty. Understanding parking logistics promotes easier travel and increases your entire experience in this dynamic city, whether you're parking by the seaside to take up the sun or traversing markets for local treasures.

Essential Contacts and Websites

As you go on your Goa excursion, having access to important connections and trustworthy websites might be helpful for a smooth journey. Here's a thorough list of contacts and resources to help you with your research:

Emergency Contacts
Police: Dial 100 for immediate police assistance in case of emergencies.

Medical Emergencies: For medical help, dial 108 or visit the nearest hospital. Additionally, having your country's embassy or consulate contact saved can be useful.

Local Tourism Offices
Goa Tourism: The official website of Goa Tourism provides information on attractions, events, and travel tips. Website: www.goa-tourism.com

Transportation Services

Goa Public Transport Corporation (Kadamba Transport Corporation): For bus schedules and routes, visit their website: www.ktclgoa.com

Accommodation Booking Platforms
Booking.com: An extensive platform for booking accommodations of all types. Website: www.booking.com

Agoda: Another reliable platform for accommodation bookings. Website: www.agoda.com

Emergency Medical Assistance
Apollo Hospitals, Goa: A well-equipped medical facility. Contact: +91-832-6721331. Website: www.apollohospitals.com

Manipal Hospitals, Goa: Renowned hospital with various medical services. Contact: +91-832-3005000. Website: www.manipalhospitals.com/goa

Local Media and Newspapers

The Navhind Times: A widely read English-language newspaper in Goa. Website: www.navhindtimes.in

Herald: Another prominent English daily newspaper. Website: www.heraldgoa.in

Tourist Police
Tourist Police Hotline: +91-7875756177. The tourist police assist visitors and address tourist-related concerns.

Embassies and Consulates
In case of emergencies or assistance related to your country, having the contact details of your embassy or consulate can be helpful.

Travel Apps
Google Maps: An essential tool for navigating Goa's streets and finding attractions.

Uber and Ola: Ride-hailing apps for convenient and reliable transportation.

Language Translation Apps

Apps like Google Translate can assist with communication, translating phrases and text.

Local SIM Cards

Consider getting a local SIM card for data and communication convenience. Major providers include Airtel, Vodafone, and Jio.

Social Media Groups and Forums:

Online travel forums and social media groups can provide insights, recommendations, and real-time information from fellow travelers.

Having these important connections and websites at your fingertips will allow you to make educated choices and remain connected during your trip to Goa. These tools guarantee you're well-prepared to immerse yourself in everything that Goa has to offer, whether you're looking for medical help, researching accommodations, or navigating local transit.

Maximizing Your Goa Experience on a Budget

Exploring Goa's wonders does not have to be expensive. With little smart preparation and local knowledge, you can maximize your Goa vacation while staying within your budget. Here's how to enjoy the best of Goa without breaking the bank:

Strategies for Accommodation
Off-Peak Travel: Visit during the shoulder seasons (spring and autumn), when accommodations are frequently less expensive.

Guesthouses & Homestays: Choose guesthouses or homestays for a genuine local experience at a fraction of the price of luxury hotels.

Shared Accommodations: Sharing accommodations with friends or other travelers might help you save a lot of money.

Culinary Delights

Local Eateries: Explore local eateries and street food stalls for budget-friendly yet delicious meals. Savory appetizers like bhaji-pao and Goan fish curry are reasonably priced.

Beach Shacks: Beach shacks provide fresh seafood and local cuisines and provide a beachside eating experience without the posh price tag.

Free and Low-Cost Attractions

Beach Activities: Enjoy the sun, sea, and sand for free at Goa's beautiful beaches. Swimming, tanning, and beachcombing are all free activities.

Cultural Sites: Learn about Goa's rich legacy by visiting old churches and temples, many of which have low or free admission prices.

Local Markets: Get a taste of the colorful local culture by visiting crowded markets such as Mapusa Market and

Anjuna Flea Market. These markets are a feast for the senses at a low cost.

Savings on Transportation

Public Buses: The local buses in Goa are an inexpensive method to travel about. Make use of local transportation resources to plan your itinerary.

Shared Rides: Share taxi rides or use ride-hailing apps to split transportation costs with fellow travelers.

Water and Beach Activities

DIY Water Sports: For thrill seekers, renting equipment for activities such as paddleboarding and kayaking might be less expensive than guided water sports.

Budget-Friendly Entertainment

Local Festivals: Attend local festivals and events that provide unique cultural experiences without breaking the bank.

Specials and Happy Hours:

Nightlife Deals: Many clubs and bars offer happy hour discounts and special deals, allowing you to enjoy Goa's nightlife without straining your budget.

Budget-Friendly Souvenirs
Handcrafted items such as textiles, ceramics, and jewelry may be found in local markets. Negotiating pricing may also assist you in obtaining unique things at affordable costs.

Pack Lightly and Smartly
Pack light to avoid extra baggage costs and to travel comfortably.

By using these cost-effective tactics, you may enjoy Goa's beauty, culture, and experiences without jeopardizing your financial objectives. Remember that Goa's allure is in its genuineness, and adopting the local way of life may lead to an exciting and inexpensive vacation.

Conclusion

As we come to the end of this guide's pages, you've traveled deep into the heart of Goa, discovering its many riches, from sun-kissed beaches to cultural wonders and all in between. Goa has surely captivated your interest, whether you are a sun seeker, a culture aficionado, an adventure seeker, or just a visitor seeking new vistas.

Goa's kaleidoscope of activities urges you to embrace its colorful culture, immerse yourself in its history, and revel in its natural beauty. Every minute spent here is a witness to the variety and complexity of this tropical paradise, from the rhythmic waves that caress the shores to the busy markets that come alive with colors and fragrances.

Remember the calm retreats that rejuvenated your soul, the bustling nightlife that roused your spirit, and the magnificent cuisines that thrilled your palette as you reminisce on your voyage. Embrace the memories of roaming through old churches, lounging on pristine beaches, and experiencing Goan hospitality.

Your adventure does not stop here; it is a continuing story that you will weave into the fabric of your particular journey. The chapters of this guide have served as your compass, guiding you across Goa's many options. As you go, may the memories you've made guide you back to Goa's embrace whenever wanderlust calls.

Goa becomes more than simply a destination; it becomes a part of who you are with each sunrise and sunset you see on these shores, with each laugh shared and tale given. So, whether you're relaxing beneath swaying palm trees, touring historic streets, or dancing under the stars, know that you're experiencing Goa in all its colorful splendor.

Appreciate the tapestry of experiences you've woven into your narrative here, and let Goa's charm linger in your heart long after you've departed. May your future journeys be as colorful, enlightening, and awe-inspiring as your days in this tropical paradise.

My heartfelt appreciation goes to you for allowing me to be your guide on this captivating adventure.

Larry E. Miller

Printed in Great Britain
by Amazon